FROM THE BLACK CHURCHES

A Historiographic Taxonomy of Religions in Jamaica

E. S. P. Mc Pherson B. A. (HONS.)

A&B

Publishers Group

First published 1983 by Black Iyahbinghi Press

Printed in Canada

COVER DESIGN: Art & Graphics byRas E.S.P. Mc Pherson
COVER (FRONT/BACK)ILLUSTRATION: Ras Jason Auguste "*IMPERIAL ITYOPIAN DESIGNS.*"
OTHER ILLUSTRATIONS: by Prince Junior

Library of Congress Cataloging-in-Publication Data

McPherson, E. S. P. (Everton S. P.)
From the Black Churches: a historiographic taxonomy of religions in Jamaica / E. S. P. McPherson.—[Rev., updated ed.]. / by John Henrik Clarke..
p. cm.
Includes bibliographical references and index.
ISBN 1-881316-26-7 (cloth) — ISBN 1-881316-29-1 (pbk)
1. Blacks—Jamaica—Religion. 2. Blacks—Caribbean Area—Religion.
I. Title.

BR645.J3 M39 2000. C58 00-060595
200'.89'9697292--dc21 CIP

African Studies/ Afro-Caribbean Studies; Americas Studies; History/ Jamaican History/ World Religions/ Comparative Religions/ Black Churches; Sociology; Anthropology

Author's Website: http://members.tripod.com/~rastaology
Author's E-mail: kumina@tbol.net Phone: 917-362-5493

"ORDER OF THE PRECEPTS"/
Ethio-Rastaology Educational Program, Religion No.1

10 9 8 7 6 5

A&B Publishers Group
1000 Atlantic Avenue
Brooklyn, New York
11238

Preface

Figure 1: HIS IMPERIAL MAJESTY HAILE SELASSIE I (H.I.M.)

A Rastaological Metaphysical Interpretation of Psalm 137

By the river of babylon
[: i. e. western euro-americas confu-sion/chaos],
there I & I [/We] sat down
[: i. e. were forcefully carried],
Yea, I & I wept, when I & I i-call [remembered] Zion
[i. e. K/Cush: Ethiopia/Alkebuland: Africa
I & I hanged our harps upon the willows in the midst thereof.
For there they that carried I & I away captive required of I & I [/us] a chant [/a song];
and they that wasted I & I required of I & I mirth, saying, chant us one of the chant of Ethiopia.
How shall I & I chant Haile Selassie I/The First chant in a strange land
If I forget thee, O [Ethiopia:] Jerusalem
let, I right hand forget her cunning.
If I do not i-call thee Haile Selassie I King: Rastafari
let I tongue cleave to the roof of I mouth
if prefer not Ethiopia above my chief joy
I-call, O Haile Selassie I King Rastafari,
The children of Edom
[i. e. the physical phase of man's conscious-ness:] in the day of Ethiopia;
Who said, rase it, rase it, even to the foundation thereof
O daughter of babylon, who art to be destroyed
happy shall I & I be, that rewardeth thee as thou hast served I & I
Happy shall I & I be that taketh and dasheth thy little ones against the stones

Figure 2: HAILE SELASSIE I/THE FIRST:RASTAFARI & The coming of 'Obadiah.' i.e. The Servants & Worshippers of H.I.M.

Figure 3: H.I.M. on religion

"...Since nobody can interfere in the realm of God we should tolerate and live side by side with those of other faiths.

In the mystic tradition of the different religions we have a remarkable unity of spirit. Whatever religion they may profess, they are spiritual kinsmen. While the different religions in their historic forms bind us to limited groups and militate against the development of loyalty to the world community, the mystics have already stood for the fellowship of humanity...... in harmony with the spirit of the mystics of ages gone by.

No one should question the faith of others, for no human being can judge of the ways of God..."

— His Imperial Majesty Haile Selassie 1, on, Religion.

Figure 4: The Rt. Hon. Marcus Mosiah Garvey,

D. C. L./Dr. of Civil Law - in robe of office as President General of the U. N. I. A. & A. C. L.

"Man's religion is something that we cannot eliminate from his system or destroy in him; therefore, it is folly for any man to go about attacking another man's religion, because to him it is fundamental. You may be a Christian; you may be Mohammedan; that is your religion.

...We are all entitled to our religious beliefs. Therefore any man who goes out and attacks religion, thinking he can convert men to the organisation by so doing is not helping the organisation. He is doing it more harm than good. We have reached the point where if we are to accomplish anything whatever we should have unison and accord..."

— The Rt. Hon. Marcus Mosiah Garvey, on, Religion.

Dedication

Figure 5: H.I.M. ...in Education Robes

"Loyalty inspires understanding and understanding co-operation; these are the clearest evidence of strength. But the solid basis for all lies in ***education****. It is education which allows people to live together, and makes one avoid*

the pit-falls of immorality, and induces respect for the law. Truly the attainment of these high aims is based on education, ***the helping of, people to live together, to avoid indulgence, immorality and lawless-ness****. " (my emphases.)*

— His Imperial Majesty Haile Selassie 1, on Education).

To

The Honor and Memory of All past, present and future "Ethiopianist Churches"

i. e., the **"Ethiopianist churches"** are "those African transferred and implanted 'Black Churches' in Jamaica; that independent 'Black Church Movement' of Africans and Afro-Jamaicans creole churches that broke from white control ecclesiastically.

TOWARDS
THE RESURRECTION OF I FAMILY

Joylyn/Rashida, Travis/Jahniell
Rachana/Valerie; Kibir Amlak/Empress Trejah
Shantel/Heather, Juanita

About This Book

The aim of this work is to develop the spiritual education of *My People*: to share/reveal *"aymero"*/ "knowledge" of Us - as *A People - A Nation*, by reasoning upon Our past, present and future esoteric revelations. It is Our hope that such Gnostics *"aymero"* (knowledge) will show *My People*/all Peoples that the **need** to come together is Our ultimate challenge...

Acknowledgment

This book is a reasoning upon the spiritual memory of the Ethiopian/African *Nation*. In a substantial sense it is *the Nation* itself. Our work - collectively - seeks to give a voice to *our exiled Nation's* humanity and divinity.

In this stead, I salute with **Honor** *My Beloved Sisters-&-Brothers -in-struggle*, who have helped throughout to make this work reprinted for Our Peoples in the USA and globally:

Sis. Juanita Gore;

Bro. Noah Howell Bey;

Bro. Patrick Tittle, *Attorney at Law*

Bro. Mark & Sis. Sheryl;

Bro. Alphanso (*Con Edison*/Harlem);

Sis. Angella (*Angelete Total Beauty Care*) & Family;

Bro. Heva *'Willy'* Dawson & Family;

Ras Claude (*C. J. & Sons, Inc.*); Ras *'Negus'* Robert.

September, 1999

I Hail the hundreds of students, teachers, specialists, Rastafari Rases and *'Dawtas'* (Sisters), and other Community activists of the cultural community, who - throughout my lecture tour of the USA - have urged me to reproduce/republish this work

In particular, we thank [the now late] Prof. Edward Scobie, Prof. James Small, Prof. Leonard Jefferies and Prof. Tao of City College; Bro. Peter Wilson of Columbia University (for whom *I am* his *mentor*) and Sis. Jennifer; Bro. Roy and Sis. Enid (my Mona campus - University of the West Indies, Jamaican *friends* now living in the New York); Sis. Paulette Suber of Barnard College, Columbia; Sis. Violet (my original *booking agent*); Bro. Delroy Anderson and *'Little'*/Mrs. Anderson and Family (my Jamaican childhood *friends - now living in N.Y.*); my *Brethren* Ras Berhane Maskal - *Co-Chairman of the Ethiopia Jamaica Society - New York Chapter* (*EJSNY*), and *a Founding Executive of the Ethiopian National Front (ENF)*; and Sis. Isis (from *"Isis Book Shop, Harlem"*).

I & I have to *acknowledge the wonderful* new cover design (March, 2000)]: Technical Graphics & Layout by Ras Jason Auguste - *"Imperial Ityopian Designs."*

Above all, to *The Almighty Creator of Heaven and Earth*: HAILE SELASSIE 1/THE FIRST: RASTAFARI, I give Thanks and Praises.

[1998; March 2000]

Acknowledgment to First Presentation and Publication

To *my friends* who assisted in the original presentation of this work, in **1983**: Maureen Mc Gill - especially; Kerry, Sis. Carol *'Ijahnyah'* Rey, Sisters. Sonia and Margaret, Ras Owen, Sis. Berincia - *'The African'* and Ras Patrick Bennett. *One love to you all always.*

To others who helped in the first publication of this work **in July 1988**: Mr. E. L. Ricketts (- now Principal of the Edwin Allen Comprehensive High School/E.A.C.H), Mrs. V. Taylor, and Mr. Henry, of EACH, Frankfield, Jamaica, *Give Thanks.*

To Ras Prince Junior, whose creative talent made the illutrations of this work visibly-presented; and Mr. Ricky McKenzie - who helped in the proof reading of this work: *Perfect Love*

I am duty bound also to publicly THANK Dr. - now Prof. - E. K. (Kamu - i. e. *The Silent Warrior*) Brathwaite, whose Afro-Caribbean lectures nurtured my long held *visions of the esoteric path to Rastafari,* that has led to works - as these/new Afro-Caribbean perspectives about Our Culture-History - presented here. He remains a refreshing *intellectual mentor* for me throughout this *Life's journey....*

> **"Whatever the task may be, man may begin it but he cannot complete it, unless The Almighty Creator sustains and supports him."**

H. I. M. Haile Selassie I

Glory Dawn. [November, 1989.]

Contents

List of Pictures and Illustrations

Part One: Introduction

We deem it necessary to further re-introduce **From "THE BLACK CHURCHES..."... BOOK ONE**, by referring Our readership to a number of official events, celebrations; Television and radio programs; Black Churches/Inter-denominational conferences/ lectures/ seminars; published books by the *Author*, and, or other writers; international book reviews; and taped/video productions, that deal with this said book/subject matter. They will set the tone for the subject-matter/historical truths *the readership* is about to encouter.

They are chronologically set out - and **range from December 1991 to June 6, 1998**, with the latest publication been, **September 1999**. These activities were pro-actively ignited from the shores of Jamaica from December of 1991, on-to-the-shores-of-the-USA from September of 1992, via Our coming here:

See/Listen RAS EVERTON MC PHERSON - President of the Black International Iyahbinghi Press, Chairman of the Rastafari Community Inter Faith Fellowship Council of Jamaica Committee (IFFCJ), **"ADDRESS TO THE IFFCJ: A CALL FOR AN END TO THE DISCRIMINATION AGAINST THE RASTAFARI COMMUNITY; AND THE OFFICIAL RECOGNITION, AND CONSTITUTIONAL IN CORPORATION OF THE RASTAFARI CULTURE/ FAITH AND ALL OTHER NON-RECOGNISED BLACK CHURCHES,"** (given at ***the Inaugural Launching of the IFFCJ, held at Kings House,*** Kingston, Jamaica, *December 1991*).

See/Listen RAS EVERTON MC PHERSON - *A M. Sc. Student; Historian/Political Scientist and Sociologist,* on **THE DIANE WRIGHT SHOW**, (Jamaica Broadcast Corporation TV, Half Way Tree,

Kingston, Jamaica), **(July 1992)**; also on this show were: SIS. SANDRA ALCOTT - *an Attorney-at-law*; [the now late] SIS. DAPHNEY – a former early *'Dawta'* / member of the *Youth Black Faith: Nyahbinghi Order of His Majesty*; RAS MIGUEL LORNE - *an Attorney-at-law*; BRO. JIMMY TUCKER - a former head of *the Caribbean Council of Churches* / Musician, Philosopher and Historian; RAS CARROT JARRETT - a former member of *THIRD WORLD BAND* / Drummer.

See Hans Wilhelm [Lockort.] (Introduction by Maxim J. Anderson), **The Mission The Life, Reign and Character of Haile Selassie I**, (ECA Associates Press, Bridgetown - Chesapeake - New York), 1989; 1993.

Sis. **Maxim J. Anderson**, in her Introduction while pointing out the shortcomings

> ".... Even so frequently mention is made of the Doc-.trine in order to explain the movements current position. However, to grasp the movement and its current doctrinal developments, it is essential to have at least a tentative understanding of antecedents (away from the stale cliches) which are central to the Rastafarian manifestation within *the 'New World.'* In short, the movement emerged via an ancient Ethiopian-Egyptian-Hebraic-West African religio-cultural line of descent. This 'line', from a Rastafarian analysis, led to Haile Sellasie I being seen as the physical and spiritual incarnation of that historical process at first by only a few.
>
> In making this affirmation, however, the present writer must also say that perhaps few Rastafarians would take this approach. For them the Bible is the only literary tradition to adhere to. *Others ... [F. N.] see things differently, and constantly search ancient and 'obscure' cross-cultural material for evidence of their version of the Truth. Thus it is principally the concept of the divinity of H.I.M. Haile Sellasie I that unites us.."* (my emphases.)

Her p. xxvi footnote 9 noted Our, **From "The BLACK CHURCHES...,"** *"...for 'other approaches to Rastafarian Doctrine. Currently, a growing number of Rastafarians are focusing on both Ethiopia and West Africa, notably Ghana, as a source and for current inspiration."*

Figure 6: H.I.M. in Churchical Robes

Ras E.S.P. Mc Pherson B.A. (Hons.), **RASTAFARI AND POLITICS... Modern Ethiopianism: Pan-Ethiopianization** (A Video/ Recorded Lecture given at The **African Poetry Theatre** - hosted by **Elder Bro. John Watusi**, Queens, New York, USA, **November 8, 1992**); (Video Taped by Elder Bro. John Watusi).

Ras E.S.P. Mc Pherson B.A. (Hons.), **From "THE BLACK CHURCHES..." to RASTAFARI (& AFRO-CENTRICITY),** (Two Lectures given at [the late] Prof. Edward Scobie and Prof. Leonard Jefferies, Black Studies Department, City College, New York, USA, **December 2, 1992**); (Video Taped by Hakim Karnak Amen-Ra Khemet Video Visions).

Ras E.S.P. Mc Pherson B. A. (Hons.), **"The Role of Women in the 'Black Churches' in Jamaica: From Maroonage to Rastafari,"** (A three hour Lecture given at Prof. Samad, Women's Development Studies, at *the Black Studies Department, City College, New York, USA*, **December 1992**.

Ras E.S.P. Mc Pherson B. A. (Hons.), **"The Anthro-historical Role of Family and Women in Rastafari,"** (A Lecture given at *the Anthropology Society of City College, New York, USA*, **December 1992**.

Ras E.S.P. Mc Pherson B. A. (Hons.), **"The Origins and Cultural Significance of the Rastafari Culture in the Americas,"** (A two hour lecture given to *The Black & Latino Student Movement, City College, New York, USA*, **December 1992**.

Ras E.S.P. Mc Pherson B.A. (Hons.), **MAN, NAM, I-MAN: The Womanhood of Man - The Family of the Race of Black Supremacy**, (A Video Taped Lecture presented at the **"In the Spirit of Africa" Symposium - a meeting of the Black Churches in New York**, held at Public School, Tompkins Ave., Brooklyn, New York, USA, **December 1992**; hosted by **Prof. James Small**.

Ras E.S.P. Mc Pherson B.A. (Hons.) Video Taped, **African Influence in Jamaican Religions** (Two lectures given at *the American Museum of Natural History Black History Month Celebrations*, New York, USA, **Saturday/Sunday February 27/8, 1993**); (Video Taped by Hakim Karnak Ankh-Ra Khemet Video Visions).

Ras E.S.P. Mc Pherson B.A. (Hons.) (Video/ Tapes/Text), **"RASTAFARI/RASTAOLOGY: A Ethio-Social Cosmology and Social Movement - the accumulation, pulling-together and synthesizing of African Paradigms/Black Churches in the Diaspora,"** (two Lectures given by Ras E.S.P. Mc Pherson - Founder, Co-Chairman of the Ethiopia Jamaica Society - Jamaica and New York, at **"The African Religion and Survival in the Americas"** *Student-Community Lecture series of Prof. James Small*, City College, New York, USA, **Saturday 4th, 11th of March, 1995**); (Recorded by Walter Morris, NY/ USA).

Ras E.S.P. Mc Pherson B.A. (Hons.) (Transcribed, Edited, Recorded, Introduced and Produced), **KULUNGU - TRADITIONAL RASTAFARI KUMINA SONGS, PRAYERS AND REASONING OF THE HOWELLITES THE FIRST RASTAFARI COMMUNITY VOL. 1 THE INITIATION & VOL. 2 THE HOWELLITES MEET THE NYAHBINGHI (Double C. D's)**, (Black International Iyahbinghi Press, c/o 809 East Gunhill Road, Bronx, N. Y. 10467, U.S.A.), **August 1996**.

Note Our Introduction to **KULUNGU... Vols. 1-4** is entitled, **"HONORING OUR ORIGIINAL ANCESTORS: A ROYAL ETHIOPIC SALUTE TO 'THE GONG'/THE HOWELLITES,"** subsection called **BRO. HOWELL/THE HOWELLITES**, pp. 19-20:

> ....Bro. Howell made an active move toward the creation and mobilization of this new **"Founded Religion."** [1] He left his isolation, began to approach others and sought to convince them. As he aroused these new beliefs in others, he strengthened his own

[1] See Joachim Wach, **Sociology of Religion**, (London), 1947.

convictions. Upon his return to Jamaica he formed **the Ethiopian Salvation Union**, that was later renamed **the Ethiopian Salvation Benevolent Society** [2] (and again renamed **the Ethiopian Salvation Society** in 1940/1).[3] His teachings represented a fusion of traditional Kumina and Judeo-Apostolic Christianity.

Bro. Howell is reported to have begun the preaching of Rastafari, on the Coke Methodist Church steps, in Kingston, 1933. [4] Here, he began the selling of a portrait of His Majesty Haile Selassie I, for a shilling. It is said that the subject of his first public meeting was, **"Ras Tafari, King of Abbyssinia,"** in January of 1933. Here in Kingston, Bro. Howell was met by other early leaders of the Rastafari Culture. Their degree of commitment to the Worship of His Majesty was just as high and intense, but their interpretations and liturgical orientations differed from his own. **Bro. Joseph/Josiah Nathaniel Hibbert** founded the **Ethiopian Coptic Faith** (and **the Ethiopian Coptic Church**) a Masonic lodge, which temporary engulfed some of the Howellites, while Bro. Howell was in Port Morant preaching and strengthening the rural roots of this new Movement.[5] **Bro. Archibald Henry Dunkley, King of Kings Mission** also worshipped His Majesty as *"The Returned Messiah: The Christ, but not The Al-*

---

[2] See Arthur Kitchen, "Pinnacle estate - oldest Rasta Community," **The Star**, (Mar.?) 8, p. 1979, center-spread.

[3] See A. A. Leevy, "THE LAIRD OF PINNACLE," **New Negro Voice**, Vol. 11 No. 28 April 10, 1943, p. 4; ibid, Augier, Smith, Nettleford, **The Rastafari Movement...**, p. 8; see also ibid, Shibata, **Rastafari Music in Jamaica..**, which stated that the ESS was established July and August of 1941; see also E.S.P. Mc Pherson, **"RASTA CHRONOLOGY (Complete)."**

[4] See Jimmy Carneige, **Some Aspects of Jamaica Politics: 1918-1938**, (Cultural Heritage Series Volume 4 Institute of Jamaica), 1973, p. 112. He noted that, the Rastafari "first reported activity was preaching from Coke Church steps in 1933."

[5] Ibid, Smith, Augier, Nettleford, **THE RASTAFARI MOVEMENT.../'Sixty Report'**, p. 7.

mighty Creator - as Bros. Howell and Hibbert firstly proclaimed." [6]

It was here in Kingston also, that Bro. Howell was to meet one his first and most loyal lieutenants, in the historical and illustrious figure of **Bro. Robert Hinds,**[7] **a former Bedwardite Lieutenant** who was arrested in the famous *Bedward People March of 1921*, and a former Garveyite. [8]

By April of 1933 Bro. Howell shifted his preaching from Kingston to the eastern parish of St. Thomas, in April 1933. [9] It is here in St. Thomas that Jamaica - through the press - was to hear of the Rastafari Movement for the first time. Resulting from one his numerous meetings that drew hundreds of the laboring classes and peasantry, [10] Bro. Howell was charged for **"words of a seditious nature,"** delivered on April 18th. **The Daily Gleaner**, reported that [in a Dec. 16th meeting] Bro. Howell's *"devilish attacks are made at these meetings on government, both local and imperial, and the whole conduct of the meeting* **would tend to provoke an insurrection if taken seriously**." [11]

---

[6] Op.cit, p.6; ibid, "DREAD HISTORY..," **REGGAE & AFRICAN BEAT**, p.20.

[7] Ibid, **'Sixty Report'**, pp.6-7.

[8] See E.S.P. Mc Pherson, **"BROTHER BEDWARD,"** (Black International Iyahbinghi Press, Frankfield P. O., Clarendon, Jamaica), March 984; rpt. April 1984; see also E.S.P. Mc Pherson, **"BROTHER BEDEWARD - A Reason Presented By E.S.P. Mc Pherson B.A. (Hons.) (U.W.I.), at the Chapleton & District Historical Society - Public Meeting, Thursday 24th of May, 1984, 7.00 p.m., at Salem United Church, Chapleton, Clarendon, Jamaica**, (Black International Iyahbinghi Press Frankfield P. O., Clarendon, Jamaica), March 1985.

[9] See Dr. Robert A. Hill, "DREAD HISTORY LEONARD P.HOWELL & MILLENARIAN VISIONS IN EARLY RASTAFARI RELIGIONS," **REGGAE & AFRICAN BEAT**, August 1984, p. 20.

[10] See **The Daily Gleaner**, January 5, 1934; see also **The Daily Gleaner**, March 17, 1934; "Leonard Howell, on Trial says Ras Tafari is the returned Messiah," **The Daily Gleaner**, October 15, 1934, p. 20.

[11] See **The Gleaner**, December, 1933.

> Officers who tried to infiltrate the meeting at Seaforth Town finally arrested Howell on a charge of sedition, for in the words of the colonial State, Howell abused the British Sovereign and Governor of Jamaica: ***"...thereby intending to excite hatred and contempt for his majesty the King of England and of those responsible for the government of the island, and to create disaffection among the subjects of his majesty in this island and to disturb the public peace and tranquillity of the island."*** [12] (my emphases.)

See also Ras E.S.P. Mc Pherson B.A. (Hons.), (Edited), **ETHIOPIA JAMAICA SOCIETY - NEW YORK**, Circular No. 1 July 1996, entitled: **"KULUNGU..." - A ROYAL ETHIOPIC SALUTE TO THE BATTLE OF ADOWA CENTENARY CELEBRATION AND BRO. L. P. HOWELL/THE HOWELLITES**, especially, pp. 17-18: [Dr.] Ken Bilby's review of KULUNGU... in **THE BEAT**, Vol. 15 #3, 1996, pp. 76-77:

> ".... Now, with the release of **Kulungu**, the Howellites-kumina connections are finally being celebrated on a medium designed to reach wider audiences. Compiled and published by Rastafari scholar Everton Mc Pherson, this two-c.d. set (soon to be joined by two volumes) represents a crucial breakthrough for the Howellites perspective. Here, for the first time, Howellites go on record about their worldview and the foundational role of their theology with its kumina roots, in the development of the movement.
>
> Ras Everton is determined to educate his Rastafari brethren and sistren and others around the world about the largely ignored page in history of the movement. All the evidence of kumina influence is here, in the Howellites drumming, chanting and reasoning preserved for posterity on these recordings. Along with the box set **[Jewel box]** Mc Pherson in-

[12] See **The Daily Gleaner**, March 14, 1934.

cludes a 68-page [**72 pages**] introduction giving historical background on Leonard Howell and discussing the place of kumina in early Rastafari theology and music. Scholars of both Rastafari and kumina will find much that is debatable here; but the overall case Mc Pherson makes for the importance of kumina in the development of Rastafari is indisputable. The package also comes with two separate booklets containing transcriptions of the spoken passages and most of the songs on the cds. These are invaluable aids to comprehension....

...anyone seriously interested in the history of reggae will want to hear these rare recordings for their hints of great things to come; here in the historical cradles of Rastafari we find clear evidence of the underground Revival-Poco [-**Puku**] and kumina roots fed into Nyahbinghi and have resurfaced in every incarnation of Jamaican popular music from ska through dancehall....

With this project, Ras Mc Pherson joins a handful of others in the Rastafari community who have begun to give recognition to their kumina roots. Another is drummer junior 'Gabu' Wedderburn, who, with his New York- based troupe, Ancient Vibrations, has been performing kumina alongside Revival, Nyahbinghi and reggae for years. *This reclamation of kumina raises unresolved questions, for the majority of Rastafari still see the invocation of ancestral spirits that is central kumina as problematic.* But in St. Thomas parish, where the Kongo-based religion and cosmology of kumina have remained most vital, local Rastas, some of them brought up in the kumina tradition, tend to have a more subtle view of kumina. Some even attended both kumina and Nyahbinghi gatherings, arguing that kumina link them to their Kongo ancestors and Africa, and are not incompatible with worshipping His Majesty. The Rasta pioneers at Pinnacle would no doubt have agreed with them.

In reclaiming kumina as a forgotten part of Rastafari history, **Kulungu** pays long-overdue homage to the African heart and soul of Jamaica. To paraphrase Marcus Garvey: 'A nation without knowledge of its history is like a tree without roots.' And for the moment, there is no better way for a broader public to gain access to the untold cultural history of Rastafari than through this unique package.

See Norman Weinstein, "vault discoveries," **Pulse** (*reggae*), December 1996, p. 30, section called GIFT IDEAS:

"These holiday gifts offer reggae's past and future. 1) **Kulungu** (Black International Iyahbinghi Press/RAS RECORDS distribution) is a two-disc box of field recordings illuminating dramatically reggae's African spiritual and musical roots..."

Ras E.S.P. Mc Pherson - Founder, Co-Chairman of the Ethiopia Jamaica Society (EJS) - Jamaica and New York; Negusa Nagast (Deputy Grand Master) of the Queen of Sheba & Pharaohs Masonic Movement - Education and Research Foundation (QSPMM) (Taped/Video), **"Black Churches: 'Black Baptists' and the Coming of Rastafari"** - *A Lecture given at the Gloria Wise Boys and Girls Club YAC-Beacon MS 113 in collaboration with the Richard Greene Middle School Presentation of* **'THE LIVING MUSEUM A Journey Through The African Diaspora'**, ***Saturday, February 24th, 1996***, *3710 Barnes Avenue, Bronx, New York 10467, U.S.A.).*

Ras E.S.P. Mc Pherson B.A. (Hons.) (Founder, Co-Chairman of the Ethiopia Jamaica Society - New York Chapter; Co-Chairman of Mo-Anbessa (The Conquering Lion Organizing Committee); Founder, Chairman of the Ethiopian National Front; Negusa Nagast (Deputy Grand Master) of the Queen of Sheba & Pharaohs Masonic Movement - Education & Research Foundation), **The Role of the Revolutionary Ethiopi-**

anist Intellectual: Prescriptives for A Paradigm-Shift Towards "The New Education"(inclusive of RASTAOLOGY) *(A Paper presented at the NATIONAL CONFERENCE on AFRICAN CENTERED EDUCATION September 30, October [1],* **2**, *1994 City College, New York City THEME: 'The Vision, Implementation and Impact of African Centered Education', Sponsored by: The Black Studies Department, City College of New York; The Coalition of African Centered Educators; and The Association for the Study of Classical African Civilizations Eastern Region)*, (A BATTLE OF ADOWA CENTENARY CELEBRATION - March 1896-March 1996/7 PUBLICATION, No. 2 An Ethiopian National Front (ENF) – Education & Research, Arts & Science Foundation Inc.; Ethiopia Jamaica Society - New York Chapter (EJSNY) Ethio-Rastaology Study Group Series, A.ORDER OF THE PRECEPTS" / Educational Program Published by the Ethiopian/Black International Iyahbinghi Press, **Sept. 1994**; reprinted Oct. 1994; republished March 1995; **September 1999**, subsection called: **THE ETHIO-RASTA CHALLENGE & CHARGE**:

> .....Before I step a bit further, I have to inform You My Khemetic/African-American Brothers and Sisters that We - the Rastafari International Community have long been following: studying and analyzing the African-American national and international struggles. In that stead, We have read a number of white American and African-American Scholars views on the Rastafari Movement. The four most profound ones are:
>
> 1) Obviously, the first academic research done on the Rastafari Movement - by a white American scholar, **George Eaton Simpson**, in 1955, [13] remains

---

[13] See George Eaton Simpson, "The Ras Tafari Movement in Jamaica: a study of race and class conflict," (Baltimore Md.), 1955; in **Social Force**, Vol. 34, Dec. 1955, pp. 167-70; see also George Eaton Simpson, "Political Cultism in West Kingston," **Social and Economic Studies**, Vol. 4 No. 2 1955, pp. 133-149, which is also in his, **Religious Cults in the Caribbean**, (University of Puerto Rico), 1970, as "The Ras Tafari Movement," pp. 208-223; see George Eaton Simpson, "The Ras Tafari Movement in Jamaica in its Millennial Aspects," **Comparative Studies in Society**

culturally significant, within the recollection of the Rastafari evolving histography.

2) [The now late] St. C. Drake's, **The redemption of Africa and Black religion**, who traced the "Ethiopianism of old," into the modern Pan-Africanist era, and unto Rastafari:

"...After 1900 Pan-Africanism gradually became the dominant political myth of the black world-replacing the Ethiopianist pre-political myth. But Ethiopianism was by no means dead. It had persisted in its oldest and most theological form in **the churches of the unsophisticated**..." (my emphases.)[15]

---

and History, Supplement 11 (1962), pp. 1160-1165, which is also in: ibid, **Religious Cults in the Caribbean**, pp. 224-228; see George Eaton Simpson, "Jamaica Revivalist Cults," **Social and Economic Studies**, Vol. 5 No. 4, 1956; see George Eaton Simpson, **Racial and Cultural Minorities**, (New York; Harper and Row), 1974; and George Eaton Simpson's latest work on the Rastafari Religion/Movement, "Religion and Justice: some reflections on the Rastafari movement," **Phylon**, Vol. 46 No. 4 (Dec. 1985), pp. 286-291.

[14] See George Eaton Simpson, "The Ras Tafari Movement in Jamaica: a study of race and class conflict," (Baltimore Md.), 1955; in **Social Force**, Vol. 34, Dec. 1955, pp. 167-70; see also George Eaton Simpson, "Political Cultism in West Kingston," **Social and Economic Studies**, Vol. 4 No. 2 1955, pp. 133-149, which is also in his, **Religious Cults in the Caribbean**, (University of Puerto Rico), 1970, as "The Ras Tafari Movement," pp. 208-223; see George Eaton Simpson, "The Ras Tafari Movement in Jamaica in its Millennial Aspects," **Comparative Studies in Society and History**, Supplement 11 (1962), pp. 1160-1165, which is also in: ibid, **Religious Cults in the Caribbean**, pp. 224-228; see George Eaton Simpson, "Jamaica Revivalist Cults," **Social and Economic Studies**, Vol. 5 No. 4, 1956; see George Eaton Simpson, **Racial and Cultural Minorities**, (New York; Harper and Row), 1974; and George Eaton Simpson's latest work on the Rastafari Religion/Movement, "Religion and Justice: some reflections on the Rastafari movement," **Phylon**, Vol. 46 No. 4 (Dec. 1985), pp. 286-291.

[15] (Third World Atlanta, Georgia), 1975 pp. 74-75. And note his section entitled: **"Edward Wilmot Blyden: Intellectual Ethiopianist,"** pp. 54-70; in ibid, Mc Pherson, **RASTAFARI and POLITICS...**, pp. 221-222. See also Edward W. Blyden, LL.D. (with an introduction by the Hon. Samuel Lewis), **CHRISTIANITY, ISLAM and the NEGRO RACE**, (London W. B. Whittingham & Co. 91 Gracechurch Street), 1887.

3) Ali Mazuri's, "Religious Alternatives in the Black Diaspora: From Malcolm X to the Rastafari," **Caribbean Affairs**, Jan.-Mar. 1990 No. 1 Vol. 3, pp. 157-160.

This works most definitively makes that trilectical link We previously spoke about; and declares that the origins and nature of the Rastafari Movement amounts to a Pharaohic and Pre-Judaic one. [16] (A key historical point, that many of Our Brothers and Sisters within Our Community are NOW just affirming in their minds and practicing in their liturgical sources of Worshipping Haile Selassie The First.)

The fact that it was **Bro. Joseph/Josiah Nathaniel Hibbert - a former President of the UNIA Local 21, in Costa Rico and a Early Founder of the Rastafari Culture - who brought African/ Khemetic Freemasonry to Jamaica**, should have made this historical roots evident. But it has represented one of those tabooed subjects by the Jamaican/Caribbean society, that remains haunted by any form of pure African cultural practices/art forms, as **African Freemasonry**, **Kumina** and the Ashanti Cosmology: **"OBI"** (corruptly called: *'obeah'*) represents......... [17]

---

[16] For one of the first African-American Scholars that first qualified the Rastafari Movement as Khemetic/Pre-Judaic in its collective origin, see G. K Oseki LL.M., Ph.D., **The Truth About the Rastafarians**, (University Place Bookshop, 821 Broadway, New York City, N.Y. 10003), April 1979, pp. 19-25.

[17] Ibid, Mc Pherson, **From "THE BLACK CHURCHES...."**

Figure 7: The Rt. Hon. Bro. J. N. Hibbert, Grand Master in Ethio-Rastafari Masonic garment

Ras E.S.P. Mc Pherson B. A. (Hons.) Founder, Chairman of The Ethiopian National Front (ENF) – Education & Research, Arts & Science Foundation, Inc.; Co-Chairman of Moa-Anbessa (The Conquering Lion Organizing Committee) (USA-N.Y./Jamaica); Negusa Nagast [Deputy Grand Master] of The Queen of Sheba & Pharaohs Masonic Movement (QS&PMM) – Education & Research Foundation; Founder, Co-Chairman of The Ethiopia Jamaica Society – New York Chapter (EJSNY); Ilect [Elect] of Throne of The Nyahbinghi Order of His Majesty Rastafari International Co-ordinating Working Committee (R. I. C. W. C.);Chairman of The Ethiopian Holocaust Remembrance Committee - New York Chapter (EHRC-NY), **RASTAFARI/RASTAOLOGY:CULTURE, IDEOLOGY, POWER, & KNOWLEDGE. Towards the Development of "The New Education" (/an 'African-American') Curricula** *(A Paper Presented to The Board of Education Title One Education Committee,* Hyatt Hotel, Brunswick, New Jersey, New York City, U.S.A., Saturday June 6th, 1998)

Ras E.S.P. Mc Pherson - Founder, Co-Chairman of the Ethiopia Jamaica Society (EJS) - Jamaica and New York; Negusa Nagast (Deputy Grand Master) of the Queen of Sheba & Pharaohs Masonic Movement - Education and Research Foundation (QSPMM), **"RASTAFARI/ RASTAOLOGY: A Ethio-Social Cosmology and Social Movement - the accumulation, pulling-together and synthesizing of African Paradigms/Black Churches in the Diaspora,"** (Two Lectures given at **"The African Religion and Survival in the Americas"** *Student-Community Lecture series of Prof. James Small, City College, New York,* ***Saturday 4th, 11th of March, 1995****)*;

Ras E.S.P. Mc Pherson B.A. (Hons.), FOUNDER, CO-CHAIRMAN OF THE ETHIOPIA JAMAICA SOCIETY (EJS) - NEW YORK CHAPTER (EJSNY); CO-CHAIRMAN OF MO-ANBESSA (THE CONQUERING LION ORGANIZING COMMITTEE); Founder, Chairman of THE ETHIOPIAN NATIONAL FRONT (ENF); and THE QUEEN OF SHEBA & PHARAOHS MASONIC MOVEMENT - EDUCATION & RESEARCHFOUNDATION (QS&PMM), **HAILE SELASSIE I IS "THE FIRE OF THE ATOM": RASTAFARI IN AMENTA/THE AMERICAS. (\"RASTAFARI AND THE AFRICAN-AMERICAN COMMUNITY: TOWARDS THE YEAR 2000 & BEYOND")**, (A Lecture sponsored by *THE NYAUVI ASSOCIATION (i.e. Together We Conqueror) of Hunter College, at Hunter College* - Thomas Hunter Hall Room [202], **Thursday March 27, 1997**, 4:00 p.m.

Introduction to the First Edition

From **"THE BLACK CHURCHES..."** is taken from a University of the West Indies, Mona campus, Jamaica, History Department Master. of Philosophy/M. Phil. Qualifying project paper. It was then fully titled: **From "THE BLACK CHURCHES" To "THE NYAHBINGHI ORDER: THE YOUTH BLACK FAITH,"** *(May 1983)*. The subject topic chosen was: **"Obeah as a Black Church."**

Throughout my earlier researches on the Black Churches in Jamaica, I noted that "obeah" permeated the history and psyche of past and present Jamaican society.

We utilized both literate and oral sources in the academia, and the urban and rural communities. We discovered that "obeah" haunted the *'cultural censors'* of the slave era, as the planter class legislators/assemblymen, their allies of the late-come *'orthodox Christianity'*: Euro-Americans and their *'overlords'* in Britain.

Obeah continued in to the post emancipation times to haunt the psyche of the then existing contemporary churches and society. Today, obeah still continues to haunt the plethora of churches in Jamaica.

It is for this reason, why, the paper was titled: **From "THE BLACK CHURCHES ...."**

The original paper looked within the mosaic array of "Black Churches" throughout the religious histography of Jamaica's existence (since slavery) which stretched in breath **from Obeah to the Rastafari Faith**.

This **"BOOK ONE"** presents a section of such a histography, from **Obeah to Bedward**, that looks at **Obeah, Myal, orthodox Christianity** (especially **the "Black Baptists"**), **Ku-**

mina, Revival (Puku and **Zion), Bedwardites** and **Higginism.**

This **"BOOK ONE,"** represents the earliest past of Jamaica's [- and the USA based and transplanted - ***Protestantised – "Black Baptist"***] religious histography. Such a religious histography and taxonomy of **Black Churches** ***need*** to be penetrated. Not only as it relates to "obeah," but as it relates to the general historical emergence and development of *exiled* Africans in Jamaica.

The presentation of these Black Churches needs precise etymological presentation. This we have done, along with presenting the related psycho-socio-cultural interpretations of the respective historical periods.

Thus I have renamed this work: **From "THE BLACK CHURCHES..." - A Historiographic Taxonomy of Religions in Jamaica.**

This **"BOOK ONE,"** makes explicit the point that: any of these respective Black Churches merits separate wholistic study. This has been done in a partial sense, for Myal by Monica Schuler; [1] for Kumina by Prof. E. K. Brathwaite; [2] for Revival by Edward Seaga; [3] and, for **"Bro. Bedward"** by *the Author.* [4]

In presenting this work, we aim to provide a wholistic reference base for further studies upon the religious matrix of

---

[1] See Monica Schuler, **"Alas Alas Kongo" - A social history of Indentured African Immigration into Jamaica, 1841 - 1865**, (The John Hopkins U. I.), 1980.

[2] See Edward Kamau Brathwaite, "Kumina - The Spirit of African Survival," **Jamaica Journal**, no. 42, pp. 44-63.

[3] See Edward Seaga, "Revival Cults in Jamaica Notes towards a sociology of religion," (reprinted from **Jamaica Journal,** Vol. 3 No. 2 June 1969).

[4] See E.S.P. Mc Pherson, **"Brother Bedward,"** (Black International lyahbinghi Press, Frankfield P.O. Box 15, Clarendon, Jamaica), March 1984, April 1984 2nd printing; see also E.S.P. Mc Pherson, **"Brother Bedward" - A Reason presented by E.S. P. Mc Pherson B.A. (Hons.) (UWI) at the Chapleton and District Historical Society - Public meeting, Thursday 24th of May, 1984,7.00 p.m. at Salem United Church, Chapleton, Jamaica**, (Black International Iyahbinghi Press, Frankfield P. O., Clarendon, Jamaica), March 1985.

Our People in Jamaica (and throughout the Caribbean) [***and the Americas***]. In the main - we aim to inform ones by analytically describing *the spiritual essence of the culture-history of Jamaica*.

It is the *author's* view that a comparative religious approach MUST be incorporated by the **CXC (Caribbean Examination Center) History Syllabus** [***and the USA developing African-centered curriculum***]. **From "THE BLACK CHURCHES..."** employs and presents such a comparative method.

This book fulfills the objectives of such a **CXC Syllabus** [/***USA multicultural curriculum***] and gives: *"knowledge"* to assist *"understanding and interpretation"*; *"analysis and evaluation"*; while sharpening the spirit of *"enquiry"* in teachers and students for maximum *"communication"* of historical data.[5]

This work touches upon many related themes of the CXC syllabus. The main ones been:

"Religion as a social force" / "Indigenous religious forms";
"Resistance and Revolt" ;
"Art forms in the Caribbean";
"The Haitian Revolution and its effect";
"Movements towards Emancipation";
"Social Life 1838-1938";
and, *"Sugar and Slavery."*

This presentation is a *primary source* directed at local tertiary institutions as: the University of the West Indies; Teachers Colleges; the United Theological College; and ***tertiary institutions internationally*** . It will richly add to the various disciplines.

To the history, sociology, anthropology and religious departments - respectively; and to the churches, established and non-established, that are schismatically squabbling among themselves this work says:

---

[5] See **"Syllabus for examination in Caribbean history,"** Objectives of the Syllabus, p. 2; Theme, p.3; **CXC History, part 3, Easter term (Radio teacher guide)**.

Our African roots are rooted in "spirituality": (religion) "Black Churches";

i) **For our contemporary development, the Churches - all Churches - have to be the main "infrastructure" and praxis of Our development as A People/society;**

ii) **There must be a due recognition of The "Black Churches," non-established churches, for "The Universal Church" to be a reality. Because no one church (/denomination) has a monopoly on the Godhead; God is not the author of confusion!**

There must be an extension by *the society-at-large* in (and throughout *the Americas*) of "the plutocratic-vision" / "plurality of vision" – to the spiritual realms.

They existed, and still exist, a diversified array of Black Churches: African and Afro-Caribbean religions in Jamaica!

The present *'trustee leadership'* must end this facade of *the "plural-myth"*: *the system* needs to demystify itself. Upon so doing, they will be able to see Black Churches, non-established churches, unincorporated churches (as Rastafari and Bedwardites) are un-apologetically racial conscious and are ideologically African cultural nationalists. Notwithstanding, these Black Churches provide service to a multiracial laity/worshippers - at times.

These un-incorporated churches ***are "racist"*** (i. e. they are - *lovers of their Race*/"racially conscious"), via preaching a "racial message": a Race-First doctrine and philosophy

So then, our established school curricula must stop the facade of *'teaching scriptures/B. K. / religion'*: i. e. the exclusive teaching of Christianity; of *'God and Jesus'*: i. e., **Euro-Western-Christianity**.

Instead, *"religious education"* must henceforth be the educating and edifying of *Our People: Children* of "Christianity" in combination with World religions: as the **KMT/Khemetic Cosmology**; **(Ethio-) Christianity**; **Judaism**; **Hindu**; **Islam**; **Buddhism**; etc.

And this MUST be anchored in the history of local religions, as **Obeah**; **Myal**; **Kumina**; **Revival**; **Bedwardism**; **Higginism**; and the **Masonic Orientations**, of *The Rt. Hon. Saint Marcus Mosiah Garvey* -- **The United Negro Improvement Association & African Communities League (UNIA & ACL) - "African Orthodox Church** (AOC)"; and **Rastafari**.

This MUST be further combined with knowledge of regional Black Churches as: **Vodun** in Haiti, **Shango** in Trinidad, **Big Drum** in Grenada, Muslim and **Hindu** in Trinidad and Guyana; **Garifuna** in Belize; and **Zombie** in Brazil etc..

These are all valid and authentic within themselves to be absorbed by the academia. Such will represent the true symbol and blossoming of "Education."

We are emphasizing the need for an interdenominational approach: the establishment of an ecumenical community by the churches, we are advocating for a universal religious comparative approach educationally to be accepted by all. Not only academicians; but, in particular, trained theologians and inspired "specialists," [6]

> *"This is so as cultural history is a set of complex factors and cannot be accounted for by [a] single monotheistic principle."* [7]

Moreover with Africans coming to Jamaica (and *'the New World'*) from geographically diversified sections of Africa, each cultural-area had its own respective dialectical socio-religious-cultural complex, and thus there would naturally exist a pantheon of religious expression in Jamaica.[8] The Akan ethnic group dominance in Jamaica and their absorption of

---

[6] See John S. Mbiti, **African Religions and Philosophy**, (Anchor Books-Doubleday and Co. Inc., Garden City, New York), e. g., pp. 258-265.

[7] See Professor Mervyn Alleyne, **"The history of African religion in Jamaica, paper presented at the Fifteenth Conference of Caribbean Historians, UWI, Mona, Jamaica, April 15-20, 1983,"** p. 2.

[8] Ibid, Alleyne, pp. 3-4 related to the factor of "diversities."

other African nationalities - linguistically and culturally, [9] resulted in "syncretism"; a "synthesis"; or blend: "Creolization." It is from this process of an African/European syncretism, Obeah and Myal - religiously emerged - respectively.

It is a fact that, "...the particular appeal of Akan magic (obeah) may have led to the adaptation of Akan religion outside the strict Akan group and that Akan themselves were willing to receive deities from other group...," as, "...happened throughout Afro- America." [10]

Obeah, then, must be seen as a **"revitalization movement,"** that radically denounced the European-imposed-fate of Africans - as slaves - captives - raped and uprooted from *Our ancestral homeland*. Africans were forcefully carried to a new environ: an alien cultural sphere: the Jamaican plantation, which had, "its own religion and array of Gods and 'divinities.'" [11]

---

[9] Op. cit, p. 4. Also, from **Lecture Notes of Dr Robatham, Anthropology, 1986-7**. He stated:

> "In the first period of slavery, Akan type influence was more in 1750s - 60s. Akans are a matrilineal influenced people. In the second period of slavery, it was a time of Ebo and Bantu type influence. The Bantu people are very strongly matrilineal and the Ebos were patrilineal. Ebos and Bantu rose to over half of the inputs into slavery."

For this and more demographic information see Barry Higman, Slave **population and economy in Jamaica**. He noted that it is from the Bantu influence that Kumina arose in Jamaica.

[10] Ibid, Alleyne, pp. 6-7.

[11] Ibid, Alleyne, pp. 13-4:

> "... Although serious Christian missionary work did not begin in Jamaica until towards the end of the 18th century, African slaves had begun experiencing the power of the European god immediately on their arrival in the island. For example, it was generally agreed that the destruction of Port Royal by the earthquake of 1694 was in accordance with the judgement of God brought down on the city for its wickedness. In fact the first law passed after the earthquake, with the preamble acknowledging that 'it has pleased God justly to punish the inhabitants of this island for the manifold sins and wickedness committed against his Divine Majesty' (Gardner 1873: 193 citing **Laws of Jamaica vol. 1**). The frequent hurricanes and other earthquakes, all attributed by the Euro-

Here on the plantation, these **Africans** - <u>called *'slaves'*</u> - created an **"alter-native"** using the **"Mask"** of "re-integration" (pretending to be 'acculturated') into the plantocracy social realm, e. g. *"Slave Drivers"* like Tacky; and *"Daddy Deacons"* like Sam Sharpe, Paul Bogle, George William Gordon, and Alexander Bedward; and Myalmen like Hurlock. [12] This resulted in a conscious effort to reconstruct a more satisfying culture. Such cultural action amounted to Our Ancestral Guardians being, symbols of the protection of the African personality.

Obeah then, was mistaken with Myal as being one and the same. Both represented a religion; a cultural system; a way of worship. It was a predominantly collective phenomena, harnessing the "collective consciousness," while seeking "collective salvation," to consciously reconstruct a more satisfying culture [13] and "a new millennium movement" on the psychic and socio-political levels of liberation, of individuals and of groups.

---

pean population to the vengeful work of the Christian god must have created a deep impression on the religious sensitivity of African slaves. It was quite natural and expected that the European god would have been adopted 'into the pantheon and into the religion of the African slaves, especially as that god possessed qualities that matched those of African deities. In addition, the Christian god was often pitted against the spiritual powers of obeahmen and myalmen, and in some cases seemed to have won out, such as when myalmen and obeahmen were caught after plotting and carrying out revolts and were put to death, their claims to invulnerability being thereby invalidated..."

[12] See E. K. Brathwaite, **"The rebellion in the Great River Valley of St James 1831/32,"** (Mona UWI), Feb. 1982; see also Monica Schuler (edited by Margaret Crahan and Frank Knight), **Myalism and the African religious tradition in Jamaica, in Africa and the Caribbean: The legacies of a link,** (Baltimore, John Hopkins University Press), 1979.

[13] Upon "the revitalization theory"/debate, see A. F. C. Wallace, Revitalization movements, in **American Anthropologist**, 1958, pp. 264-281; see also Klaus De Albuquerque, **Millenarian movements and the politics of liberation: the Rastafarians of Jamaica**, (Virginia Polytechnic Institute and State University, Ph.D.) 1977 Sociology, general, pp. 433-4; see Barry Chevannes, **Social Origins of the Rastafari Movement**, (Institute of Social and Economic Research, UWI, Mona), 1978, p. 4.

Albuquerque's book is most instructive on "Millenarian movements ."

It was symbolic of the discarding of the old self (i. e. the early period of slaves coming to Jamaica). This was a period which was marked by "tribal religious fragmentation," reactionary fatalistic acts of suicidal tendencies, and recriminations among slaves. It resulted in "witchcraft" and selected "anti-social" aspects of African religion upon each other.

This resulted in the continuing uprisings, to recreate traditional African religion/society, as was seen by Tacky's 1760 revolt, and the Kenecuffes: Maroons War of liberation, e. g. Nanny war upon the plantocracy.

There were later African cultural retensions and religious resurgence as a Myal Pan-Black-Front that syncretized with orthodox Christianity. This was so especially with the 'Black Baptists', e. g., in the 1831/32 Baptist-Myal War.

What religion represented to the slaves was a central symbol for integration of values: communal life and social order, day-to-day collective sacralization. [14]

The Black Church became a cultural symbol; a means of collective transpersonal communication; [16] an instrument used for resistance and revolt, group cohesion and identity!

It is the beginning of this religious histography that accounts for many readers' view/the academia fundamental misunderstanding of the development of religions in Jamaica. Whereby, many still tend to confuse Obeah with Myal, and further confuse both with "witchcraft." [18]

---

[14] See Max Assimeng, "Crisis, identity and integration in African religion," Hans Mol's (Edited), **Identity and Religion International, Cross Cultural Approaches**, (Sage Studies in International Sociology 16/1. S. Association), 1978, p. 99.

[15] See Max Assimeng, "Crisis, identity and integration in African religion," Hans Mol's (Edited), **Identity and Religion International, Cross Cultural Approaches**, (Sage Studies in International Sociology 16/1. S. Association), 1978, p. 99.

[16] See for example Olive Lewin, "Underlying values in traditional communication," **Communications and information for development purposes in the Caribbean area**, (Georgetown, Guyana, 1-8 December, 1974), pp. l6-19.

[17] Op. cit.

[18] Ibid, Alleyne, pp. 10-ll:

> "The emphasis in the literature on obeah was certainly part of the inability and unwillingness of the European establishment to understand the culture of Africans. It is however probable that conditions in slavery, i. e. mainly the proscription of religious assemblies of slaves and the need to mobilise the spiritual force of resistance and survival, led to the greater dominance of obeah over other forms and components of the slaves' religion. In fact, it may be significant that the original Ashanti name of the sorcerer Obayifo was continued in the term obeah, whereas the name of his counterpart, the priest Okomfo was not continued and gave way quite early to the term myalman, based, it is alleged, on the name of the dance myal.
>
> There was, and still is, considerable confusion over the terms 'myalism' and 'obeah.' Some 20th century writers (Patterson, 1967, Williams, 1932 and DeLisser, 1913) have implied that the distinction between the two is fundamental to an understanding of the development of religion in Jamaica. Myalman and obeahman are terms which emerge in Jamaica to correspond to important and fundamental religious and quasi-religious activities handed down to Jamaica not only by Coromantees but virtually every ethnic group whose members found themselves in Jamaica. These are the activity of priest, and the activities that fall under the name of 'medicine man', 'witch doctor' and 'sorcerer.' In the African context it was recognised that 'good' and 'evil' are not always clearly antithetical entities. This became more pronounced in Jamaica where magic designed to bring harm to the members of the white ruling class and to slaves who showed excessive loyalty to them would exist in that nebulous grey area between 'good' and 'evil.'. ."

From Lecture **Notes of Dr Robatham, Anthropology, 1986-7**, the many ritual specialists were for example **"Bomson,"** i. e., **"priest,"** who deals with town, **"Dumsefo"** deals with health/bushes; **"Donsom kwato"** deals with evil. Also in this Ashanti culture **"evil spirits"/"witchcraft"** was **"Kumktima."** The concept underlying this cosmology was that **"good force"** as rain, sky and earth were good spirits for the **"good of the community"**; and the parts of nature that are conquered are "good," as it was from the wilderness that "evil" came. Such, was characteristic of African religions, as they are "nature-based" and this "nature religion" expresses itself by a controlled set of nature forces e. g., the earth, trees and rivers - and humans (who have several spirits). It's a concept of nature being governed by his spiritual forces, thus there are for example, **"Asaae"** power of the earth, **"Nyame"** sky god, **"Bosom,"** i. e., **children of Nyame and as human came from Ancestors having different 'souls'/"3 Genos," Ancestors are called and deified as "Samanfo."**

Upon this "Akan" cosmology, see for example J. B. Danquau (illustrated by Kofi Antubam of Achimota), **The Akan doctrine of God, A fragment of Gold**

This is due to the warped emphasis by European/Euro-oriented scholars and scholarship. They, and the local *creoles*, continue to use biased literate sources, and thus they are unable to fathom these Black Churches.

Added to this is the fact that these Black Churches met "secretly," and were "secret societies." [19]

Coast ethnic and religion, (Frank-Cass & Co. Ltd.) 1968; see also E. Bolaji Idowu, **Olodumane God in Yoruba belief**, (Longmans), 1962; 1963.

See also Raffaele Pettazzon, (authorised translation by H. J. Rose), **The all-knowing god researches into early religion and culture**, p. 36:

> "...in Gold Coast, the Supreme Being (is) **'Nyongmo'** among the Ga, **'Nyankupon'** among the Tshi-speaking peoples, '(O)nyame' among the Ashanti is none other than the sky god..."

[19] Ibid, Alleyne, p. 11, pp. 8-9:

> "Two very significant factors affected the development of religion in Jamaica. First of all, up to the abolition of the slave trade, there was a continuous revitalization of African theologies by the arrival of new slaves from Africa. These new arrivals would have tended to keep alive the integrity of African religious beliefs and strengthen the adherence to traditional practice. There are numerous reports that obeahman tended to come from the ranks of African-born slaves. Secondly, very early in the history of slavery in Jamaica, laws were passed banning the assembly of slaves in great numbers on Sundays and holidays. This prohibition must have put an early end to open celebration of religion by the slaves, and thereafter, until the arrival of Christian missionaries in Jamaica, when, as we shall see, slaves were able to celebrate their religion under the guise of Christianity, and especially, until the emancipation of slaves, religious celebrations were either held in secret or became suspended. This encouraged the separation of the priest from a total structure of religious observance and led to the predominance of the obeahman operating alone. Writers of the period certainly focused on this latter personality and the literature abounds with descriptions of the obeahman and his activities. Later, of course, obeah also came under legal prohibition because it became known to the British that obeah was closely allied to slave rebellions."

[20] Ibid, Alleyne, p. 11, pp. 8-9:

> "Two very significant factors affected the development of religion in Jamaica. First of all, up to the abolition of the slave trade, there was a continuous revitalization of African theologies by the arrival of new slaves from Africa. These new arrivals would have tended to keep alive the integrity of African religious beliefs and strengthen the adherence to traditional practice. There are numerous reports that obeahman tended to come from the ranks of African-born slaves. Secondly, very early in the history of slavery in Jamaica, laws were passed banning the assem-

In other words the activities of **"Priest"** fell under the name, **"Medicine Man,"** "witch doctor" and "sorcerer," while the white's were unable to distinguish "good magic" from "evil."

This misperception about these earliest Black Churches became further compounded with the coming of **the 'Black Baptists'** from America in 1783. The resulted was that the Myalists "masked" themselves to create an array of Native Baptist churches from Sam Sharpe to Bogle and Gordon to Bedward and Higgins.

It is our hope then, that clarity will be given to the differences and similarities between Obeah and Myal; *The Spirit - "good magic"* and "witchcraft."

We are hereby giving clarity to the coming of Euro-Western Christianity; and the conscious collective process of "masked" African convert's acceptance of Christianity. [21]

---

bly of slaves in great numbers on Sundays and holidays. This prohibition must have put an early end to open celebration of religion by the slaves, and thereafter, until the arrival of Christian missionaries in Jamaica, when, as we shall see, slaves were able to celebrate their religion under the guise of Christianity, and especially, until the emancipation of slaves, religious celebrations were either held in secret or became suspended. This encouraged the separation of the priest from a total structure of religious observance and led to the predominance of the obeahman operating alone. Writers of the period certainly focused on this latter personality and the literature abounds with descriptions of the obeahman and his activities. Later, of course, obeah also came under legal prohibition because it became known to the British that obeah was closely allied to slave rebellions."

[21] Ibid, Alleyne, pp. 8-9. Read for example, Diane Robertson, Jamaican **herbs, nutrition and medicinal values,** (Ja. Herb Ltd., P. O. Box 978, Kgn., Ja.), March 1982, pp. 1-2. The *author* is not in agreement with her interpretation of who was an "obeahman"/what was "obeah." e. g. :

> "A myalist is the opposite to the 'obeah-man' who was known to use evil spirits to do harm to people. A 'myalist' had to counteract the evils of the obeahman and this was the beginning of revival and bush-baths..."

Again, "'Myalists" did not start "bush-baths." Such was from ancient times... a core-part of *"The specialist"* in Africa, known as *"The Obeahman"* in Jamaica who had long preceded "Myal.'

She, however, rightly stated:

> "Some 'educated' Jamaicans tend to forget their African origins, but the majority of our people remain close to their ancestry...
>
> Folk medicine is practised in every country at various social levels and reflect the racial environment and historical background of the people. Jamaica, like other countries, should therefore view this important part of its culture in an objective way..."

She goes on to categorize three herbal users - ***"practitioners": The Revivalist, the Obeahmen and The 'psychic' or Mother***, noting that some, .." *revivalists confine their healing to a church because of risk being confused with the 'obeahman.'"*

Here one should note that in the recently "Liberated': nations such as Zimbabwe, **"Bush Doctors"/"Healers"** have been incorporated in their country's Ministry of Health officially.

How long will *the "mask"* /hiding and deceit continue to abound within the Jamaican society, before there is an acceptance of these *"Specialists" - Inspirational Gifts of "good to mankind"* that they offer?

See for example, "Emancipation celebrations," **The Sunday Gleaner**, July 10, 1988, p. 5. Dr. Fitzroy Baptiste, lecturer in African history at the St Augustine campus (UWI)

> ".. said that the traditional shango belief, practised in Trinidad and Tobago is an offshoot of the Orisha faith of the Yorubas. This, he said, is close to Jamaican pocomania except that pocomania is Ghanaian rather than Nigerian."

[22] Ibid, Alleyne, pp. 8-9. Read for example, Diane Robertson, Jamaican **herbs, nutrition and medicinal values,** (Ja. Herb Ltd., P. O. Box 978, Kgn., Ja.), March 1982, pp. 1-2. The *author* is not in agreement with her interpretation of who was an "obeahman"/what was "obeah." e. g. :

> "A myalist is the opposite to the 'obeah-man' who was known to use evil spirits to do harm to people. A 'myalist' had to counteract the evils of the obeahman and this was the beginning of revival and bush-baths..."

Again, "'Myalists" did not start "bush-baths." Such was from ancient times... a core-part of *"The specialist"* in Africa, known as *"The Obeahman"* in Jamaica who had long preceded "Myal.'

She, however, rightly stated:

> "Some 'educated' Jamaicans tend to forget their African origins, but the majority of our people remain close to their ancestry...
>
> Folk medicine is practised in every country at various social levels and reflect the racial environment and historical background of the people. Jamaica, like other countries, should therefore view this important part of its culture in an objective way..."

We are *not* advocating the acceptance of "witchcraft" (*'obeah'* as it is confusingly called).

We are calling instead, for ones to see fit the cultural wholeness of the "Ashanti art form," now seen in *the "healer fraternity"* of present day Black Churches as Kumina, Revival and Shango, etc.

We hearken to ones to realize that this religious practice *"...of the West Coast of Africa"* dates *"directly back to Egypt"* **[Khemet/KMT]**, and that

> *"The obeah rites practised today in the West Indies had origins back with Moses..."* [23]

As I said - in my *Letter to the Editor - a contribution towards the Centenary Celebration* - that can be found in Our **APPENDIX** of this work: *ICONS as **Tacky** and **Cudjoe** should be Honored as National Heroes.* But with the unresolved specter

---

She goes on to categorize three herbal users - ***"practitioners": The Revivalist, the Obeahmen and The 'psychic' or Mother***, noting that some, .". *revivalists confine their healing to a church because of risk being confused with the 'obeahman.'"*

Here one should note that in the recently "Liberated': nations such as Zimbabwe, **"Bush Doctors"/"Healers"** have been incorporated in their country's Ministry of Health officially.

How long will *the "mask"* /hiding and deceit continue to abound within the Jamaican society, before there is an acceptance of these *"Specialists" - Inspirational Gifts of "good to mankind"* that they offer?

See for example, "Emancipation celebrations," **The Sunday Gleaner**, July 10, 1988, p. 5. Dr. Fitzroy Baptiste, lecturer in African history at the St Augustine campus (UWI)

> ".. said that the traditional shango belief, practised in Trinidad and Tobago is an offshoot of the Orisha faith of the Yorubas. This, he said, is close to Jamaican pocomania except that pocomania is Ghanaian rather than Nigerian."

[23] See Henri Gamache, **Mystery of the Long Lost 8th, 9th and 10th Books of Moses together with the legend that was of Moses and 44 secret keys to universal power**, (Sheldon Publications, Highland Falls, New York), 1967 4th printing, section called: About the tenth book the book of miscellany, Chapter 1, Origins of modern Mosaic influences or "The Great Voodoman of the Bible," p. 68, pp. 66-68.

of "Obeah" haunting the psyche of the authorities and Our People, such might be asking too much! [24]

---

[24] See E. S. P. Mc Pherson B.A. (Hons.), **The Rt. Hon. "Marcus" Mosiah Garvey, The Black Moses and St John The Divine - A Black Internationalist and "Philosophic Statesman's" Challenge to the State and Church, Educators and Our People - A Voice Crying Out In The Wilderness** (Unpublished letter to the editor) Feb., 1987, section called: **Hero "Tacky" - The ANC and PAC: Public Education Programme**:

"My other prescriptive, in addition to Dr Lewis's four and my above are:

7) 1 call upon the government to also recognize 'General' Tacky - the obeahman/priest as a National Hero. As with *'Colonel Cudjoe'*, too little is known of him and his 'inter-communal revolt' of 1760 which shook 'white society' forcing their 'cultural censors': white assembly-men on the 1st June 1760 to draft a law in the Jamaican Assembly against 'obeah' men and women.

Though his war of liberation was not successful, it should be nationally recognized. He was executed by *the plantocracy*: his head was chopped off and placed on a bamboo for viewing in the streets. Sam Sharpe's led the 1832/3: 'Baptist-Myalist-War.' He was hanged. In the aftermath of *'the Morant War'*, Paul Bogle and George William Gordon - were hanged.

Since the Tacky Revolt, the other major revolts, and most of the respective Icons are now nationally recognized. They include the matriarchal Queen Nanny: the Maroons.

Colonel Cudjoe - of the Maroons is still not recognized!

The reason why these ICONS from the pre-christian era are suppressed and are not officially recognized by the Jamaican contemporary churches, politicians and educators, is because Tacky was a Obeahman, and his Koromantees' kins were Obeahmen and Women! And as long as the specter *'obeah'* continues to haunt the Jamaican society, this *state of affair* will continue.

How many of our people know that the law drafted by the plantation against 'obeah', on the 1st of June 1760, represented the first illegal-legal arrest of Black Divinity upon the Jamaican plantation?

What, then, of the Kenecuffes Nanny and Cudjoe, the Maroons, whose traditional worship was/is 'Obi', the Ashanti traditional religion? Should they not be recognized as National Heroes and Heroines respectively?

Moreover the people should note and know, that the religious taxonomy of *'J.A.'s' /'Jamdown's'* plantation DID NOT begin with 'orthodox Christianity.' It began with pure traditional African religious forms: Obeah, then Myal - an Afro-Creole religious form.

Let us then remember, not only Cudjoe, but also Tacky in this Centenary...." (p. 7.)

Bibliography to Introduction

Albuquerque, Klaus De, **Millenarian move-meanest and the politics of liberation, the Rastafarians of Jamaica**, (Virginia Polytechnic Institute and State University, Ph.D.), 1977 Sociology, general.

Alleyne, Professor Mervyn, **"The history of African religion in Jamaica. Paper presented at the Fifteenth Conference of Caribbean Historians, UWI, Mona, Jamaica, April 15-20, 1983."**

Assimeng, Max, "Crisis, identity and integration in African religion," in Hans Mol (Edited), **Identity and Religion International, Cross-Cultural Approaches**, (Sage Studies in International Sociology/Sage Publications Inc., 275 South Beverley Drive, Beverly Hills, California 90212), 1978, pp. 97-118.

Brathwaite, E. **"The rebellion in the Great River Valley of St James, 1831/32"** (Mona, UWI), 1982.

Brathwaite, E. K., Kumina, The spirit of African survival, **Jamaica Journal**, no. 42, pp.44-63.

Chevannes, Barry, **Social Origins of the Rastafari movement**, (Institute of Social and Economic Research, UWI, Mona, Kingston) 1978.

(Crahan, Margaret and Frank Knight edited), Myalism **and the African religious tradition in Jamaica, in Africa and the Caribbean: The legacies of a link,** (Baltimore: John Hopkins University Press), 1979.

Danquau, J. B., **The Akan doctrine of God - A fragment of Gold Coast Ethic and Religion**, (illustrated by Kofi Antubam of Achi in ota), (Frank-Cass & Co. Ltd.), 1968.

"Emancipation celebrations," **The Sunday Gleaner, July** 10, 1988, p. 5B.

Gamache, Henri, **Mystery of the long lost 8th, 9th and 10th book of Moses together with the legend that was of Moses and 44**

secret keys to universal power, (Sheldon Publications, Highland Falls, New York), 1967 4th. printing.

Higman, Barry, **"The problems of slave economy in Jamaica."**

Idowu, E. Bolaji, **Olodumane God in Yoruba belief**, (Longmans), 1962

Lectures of Dr. Don Robatham, in Anthropology of the Caribbean Peoples, at Mona, UWI, Jamaica, 1986-7.

Lewin, Oliver, "Underlying values in traditional communications," **Communications and information for development purposes in the Caribbean area,** (International Broadcast Institute Ltd.) 1975 pp.16-19.

Lewis, Dr Rupert, "Marcus Garvey and Captain Cudjoe. Maroons in Jamaican literature.. . A talk given in Accompong early this year to mark the 248th anniversary of the treaty signed by Cudjoe with the British," **The Sunday Gleaner**, Feb. 15, 1987, p. 6C.

Mbiti, John S., **African religions and philosophy,** (Anchor Books-Doubleday and Co. Inc., Garden City, New York, 1976.

Mc Pherson, E.S.P., **"Brother Bedward" - A reason presented by E. S. P. Mc Pherson B.A. (Hons.) (UWI), at the Chapleton and District Historical Society - public meeting, Thursday 24th of May, 1984 7.00 p.m. at Salem United Church, Chapleton, Jamaica**, (Black International Iyahbinghi Press, Frankfield P.O., Clarendon, Jamaica), March 1985.

Mc Pherson, E.S.P., **"Brother Bedward,"** (Black International Iyahbinghi Press, Frankfield P.O., Clarendon, Jamaica), March 1984; second printing April 1984.

Mc Pherson, E.S.P., ".. **A Voice Crying Out In The Wilderness,"** (A centenary celebration paper letter to Gleaner editor, unpublished) Feb., 1987

Mol, Hans (Edited), **Identity and Religion International, Cross-Cultural Approaches**, (Sage Publications Ltd.), 1978.

Pettazzon, Raffaele (Authorised translation by H. J. Rose), **The All-Knowing God: Researches into early religions and culture**.

Robertson, Diane, **Jamaican herbs nutritional and medicinal values**, (Jamaican Herbs Ltd.), 1982.

Schuler, Monica, **"Alas Alas Kongo" - A social history of indentured African immigration into Jamaica, 1841 - 1865,** (The John Hopkins University Press), 1980.

Seaga, Edward, "Revival cults in Jamaica - Notes towards a sociology of religion" (reprinted from **Jamaica Journal**, Vol. 3 No. 2 June 1969.

"Syllabus for examination in Caribbean history, objectives of the syllabus."

Wallace, A. F. C., Revitalization movements, **American Anthropologist**, 1958, pp. 264-281.

Part Two:Original Text

Figure 8: The Rt. Hon. Bro. L.P. Powell - First Announcer of the Rastafaari Culture

"Owing to the universal rend of our ancient and modern kingdoms we are at this junction of our history scattered over the globe into little sectional groups.

All our local bands throughout the globe are bent towards King Alpha's Royal Repository, the Royal Authority is to admit all bands, mission camps, denominations into the supreme Royal Repository..." [1]

---

[1] See G. G. Maragh, **The Promise Key**, (The Harding Commercial Printry, 28 George Lane, Kingston, in Dr Nnamdi Azikiwe [Ed.], The **African Morning Post**, Head Office Accra, Gold Coast), pp. 4-5. For views upon this first primary literate source of the Rastafari histography, written by **"Brother Howell"/L. P. Howell, "The First Announcer of the Rastafari Faith,"** see also "Ginger" column, "Pepper Pot" in Jamaica **Times**, May 1938 pp. 9-10; **Jamaica Journal**, Vol. 16 No. 1, Feb.

The etymology of "Obeah"

It was Leonard Barrett who rightly stated:

> *"Both witches and wizards, priest and priestesses were brought to Jamaica in the days of the slave trade and the slaves recognised the distinction between the former and the latter."* [2]

The above distinction, along with a very insightful etymological look upon the corruption of the word **"obayi"** was noted by a writer who put it thus:

> *"The Ashanti and kindred tribes, that is, the Twi-speaking groups called Koromantyns by the slave dealers, were exported from the Gold Coast to British... colonies... Obayi, or the practice of* **witchcraft** *among those tribes, was taken to Jamaica and became the esoteric possession of the slaves which they did not share with the whites, but which nevertheless they could use for their* **personal advantage** *against their owners. The word,* **obayi**, *became corrupted into* **obeah**, **obiah** *or* **obia**, *and the form* **obi** *was also used."* [3] (my emphases.)

1983 p. 34; Ken Post, Arise **Ye Starvelings, the Jamaica Labour Rebellion of 1938 and its aftermath** (Marthus Nyhoff, The Hague/Boston/London), 1978, p. 197 footnote 51; Roy Augier, M. G. Smith and Rex Nettleford, **The Rastafari Movement in Kingston, Jamaica**, (Kingston, UWI, ISER), 1960, p. 6; and from Oral sources (Taped by E. S. P. McPherson, History Department, Mona, UWI), **The Howellites**, "Hill 60," Salt Spring, Vere, Clarendon, Jamaica, 1981-2.

[2] See Leonard Barrett, The **Sun and Drum - African roots in Jamaican folk tradition**, (Sangster Book Store Ltd., Kingston, Jamaica-Heinemann), 1976, p. 69. This quote was taken from Herbert G. Delliser, **Twentieth Century Jamaica**, (Kingston, Jamaica), 1930 p. 108.

[3] See Ivor Moorish, **Obeah, Christ and Rastaman Jamaica and its religion**, (James Clarke and Co.), 1982, p. 23. Note: highlighted words are author's em-

In Twi, **"bayi"** means **"witchcraft," "sorcery"**; and **"o-bayifo" "witch," "wizard"** (literally implying "witchcraft person"/'obeahman'). [4]

F. C. Cassidy in his, **Jamaica Talk...**, pointed out that, "The spelling obeah was Long's and has continued to be the standard one, though **obea** was formerly used and **obi** also." [5] It was also spelt **"uobia, obia, wobia, hobia"** (all meaning subject/verb word) and **"obah"** (a probable derivative from **"ubio,"** a thing or mixture of things put in the ground, as

---

phases (especially **"witchcraft"** and **"personal advantage"**). "Obeah" - in this book - is a "Black Church"; and, is seen from the perspective of its positive attributes as a "cultural tool," of **"Specialists,"** used for the **"good of mankind"**/*the community*, than for "personal advantage" - which "witchcraft" serves. This point will soon be expounded upon (and this is why footnote 2 was chosen, to show the ambiguity existing. This needs clarity, so as to reveal and distinguish **"Priest/Priestess/Specialist,"** separate from "witches/ wizards."

Moorish further noted,

> *"... that other forms of witchcraft exist in Africa and that some of those have been transmitted to the Caribbean area - particularly to Haiti and have been developed into very different sorts of cults. Ophiolatry or snake worship existed in west Africa, particularly Dahomey and southern Nigeria for a very long time. From about 1725... slaves were shipped to the West Indies from Whydah took python worship or the voodun cult with them.... But whilst the cult and the term voodoo and its variants, (vodu, voudoun) exist in Haiti and in some of the surrounding islands such as La Gonave, they have not survived in Jamaica and it seems improbable that this particular form of witchcraft or religion ever took root there..."*

While Moorish now calls such "worship"/"cults," *"a form of witchcraft or religion"*; in the Author's view, **"Religion,"** is a more "wholesome" classification for these "cultural forms."

Let us never forget, it was **"Vodun"**: "the psycho-cultural strength/*the spirit reality*," the military might and tact of **Mackandal/Boukman/Toussaint L'Ouverture,** etc. that gave the enslaved Africans their first victory over the plantation - the French West Indies. **The Haitian Revolution** represents the greatest revolutionary victory of the 19th century for diasporic People.

[4] Op. cit, p. 22: *"Obayfo"* i. e., *"vampire,"* p. 23. See also Frederic C. Cassidy, Jamaica **Talk - Three hundred years of the English language in Jamaica,** (Institute of Jamaica, London, Macmillan and Company Ltd., New York, St. Martinus Press) 1961, p. 241.

[5] Op. cit, Cassidy, p. 241.

charm to cure sicknesses or death), [6] and **"OED"** [7] gives **"efik ubio."**

Cassidy further noted *"Banbury adapted Long's etymology which went back to a Hebrew term (***0b***), the name of an ancient idol,"* [8] which (unfortunately) he says, *"cannot be supported to-*

---

[6] See F. G. Cassidy and R. E. Le Page, **Dictionary of Jamaican English**, (Cambridge University Press), 1967, p. 326.

[7] Op. cit, Cassidy and Le Page.

[8] See The Rev. R. Thomas Banbury, **Jamaican Superstition or the obeah book - A complete treatise of the absurdities believed in by the people of the island, Jamaica**, (Martiner L. De Souza, Printer 7, Church Street, Jamaica), 1894, p. 6. He noted,

> *"The word obeah or obi is said to be derived from an Hebrew term 'Ob', the name of an ancient idol and the superstition practice itself as connected with it to have taken its rise in Egypt and thence spread over the whole continent of Africa..."*

Although this was not consciously done to objectify his point. he goes on further to support the "transatlantic theory," i. e., that black culture did cross *the "salty sea,"* by stating , *"From this it is easily imagined how it reached the West Indies: the importation of slavery from that continent."*

Banbury's limited cultural knowledge and, or, Euro-oriented cultural perspective led him to describe the vehicle responsible for the transportation of this cultural form, this way :

> *"...the African obeahman carried his obeah magic with him under the hair of his head when imported. For that reason the heads of Africans were shaven before being landed, or if that was done, he swallowed the things by which he worked in Africa before leaving."*

Banbury could not have known that without the carrying of metaphysical articles/"objects," this "cultural form" was "immanently" self made, to "adapt" to/in a new environ, as "the Americas." Such a situation was for the African like the beginnings of "religion"/"worship," which in Euro-centric classification is called "animistic"/"animism" - societies/existence, in which "totemic" worship arose, as E. Durkheim's, **The Elementary form of the religious life,** (London), 1915, stated. This is a primary view of the functionalist school in (**European**) Sociology of Religion.

For example, the African transported totems of **"Anancy"** and **"the Lion,"** that energized the submerged African cultural forms in a new environ, This gave power - evident/via thoughts/ words (as in folklores etc.). See Dennis Forsythe, **West Indian culture through the prism of Rastafarism**, (Dept of Sociology, UWI, Mona), 1979 especially pp. 10-67. In subsection called **Traditional African culture**, p. 10, he stated:

day however." The word refers to the collection of things with which the obeahman works his charms, for which **"OED gives efik ubio."**

The author has found further supportive evidence to validate Banbury's argument. W. Errol Bowen's article, **"In Jamaica the occult live and it's called obeah,"** stated:

> *"...the etymology of the word obi has been traced back to ancient Egypt. A serpent in the Egyptian language was called* **'ob'** *or* **'aub'***, and Moses in the name of God forbade the Israelites to enquire of the demon, 'Ob', which is translated in the Bible as charm of wizard, divinator or sorcerer. And the so called Witch of Endor is called* **'Oub'** *or* **'Ob.'"** (my emphases.) [9]

Another supportive evidence of Banbury's point was found by the author in an article titled, **"That word obeah,"** which though not pointing to an Egyptian etymological foundation, noted:

> *"..in a book of* **Hiland Gaelie charms** *I found a word ob or oba, apparently with a long 'o', meaning 'spell' , incantation, 'charm' and there are similar words with similar*

> *"African culture tied Africans intimately to their environment and to the overwhelming order of nature within which they live. Their survival depended on their adaptation to this order... 'Animism' reflected a key in respect of faith in nature and included the belief that all objects of nature possess a natural life or vitality or are endowed with in-dwelling souls, 'a spirit' or 'secret' force..."*

Banbury's book, is an example of the "animistic and totemic symbols" at work; symbols, that are used by *the 'obeah-man'* in his *'science'/"witchcraft,"* up to this day.

[9] See Errol Bowen, **"In Jamaica the Occult lives and it's called obeah,"** (n. d.). See Celis, on pp. 8-9. She stated,

> *"The occult has been in existence for centuries, even before the birth of Christ. It was practised in Israel by Mannaseh (11 King 21: 9) though it was forbidden by the law (Lev. 19:31 and 20:6,7). It was not only under the old law that it was condemned but in the book of Acts (Ch. 19:19) we see that those who practised curious magical 'arts had their books collected and thrown into the fire' on their belief in the teaching of the gospel."*

meaning (never apparently meaning a physical object) in a tale which is perhaps earlier than 1700."

This article concluded,

"...this seem to explain how obeah became a normal English word in the Caribbean, quite early, and how amongst the slaves [10] *the word did not flourish, though in Jamaica, guzzo and related words has survived."* [11]

Obeah/ "The Obeahman"

The normative Eurocentric description/ perception of an "obeahman" was best given by Rev. Banbury,

"..he is the agent incarnate of Satan, the Simon Magus of these good gospel days; the embodiment of all that's wicked, immoral and deceptious. You may easily at times distinguish him by his sinister look, and slouching gait. An obeahman seldom looks anyone in the face... some have... been known to be decent in their appearance... He is a profes-

---

[10] Ibid, F. C. Cassidy, p. 242:

"Virtually equivalent to obeah is the word guzu. The first record of it was Russel's gasa but Beckwith spelt it goozoo. You may say 'working goozoo' as well as 'working obeah.' It has been reported in the form guszoo. The source is possibly from Twi, which has several related phrases containing guso and meaning 'to conjure', 'to do against' and so on."

[11] See H. P. J, **"That word obeah."** This article further theorizes/speculated that:

"The word, obeah, must have gone from island to island when slaves would move with their masters. Thus it probably went from Antigua to St. Vincent and from there to Trinidad, where it appears in 1803. Quite likely it came from the Eastern Caribbean. It is reported in Bermuda in 1818."

This article/author, which seems to be from Trinidad, and the assumption of obeah's earliest appearance in 1803, implies that such references were not relating to the Jamaican experience. For as early as the 1760s the word "obeah" was already within the Eurocentric literate archives of the plantation.

sional man that is well paid as the lawyer or doctor and sometimes better... .in cases of lawsuit, the obeahman is retained.

The obeahman is to be feared in the system of poisoning which he carries on... [12]

...The superstitious resort to the obeahman on every initial occasion, as well as for the purpose, of injuring others. The chief resort to the 'bushman' is to injure, either to kill outright or to afflict... [13]

It is a well known fact that the obeahman is believed to make prosperous.

...sometime application is made for the purpose of punishing thieves.

...Obeah will cause a person to do anything wicked.

... An obeahman going into any place of business can draw away as much money that he likes." [14]

"Obeah," Banbury said,

"..is made in the simplest manner possible. Anything that the obeahman can come at conveniently - piece of broken bottle, cats or serpents, teeth, nails and bones, pins, needles, vials, piece of cloth and things got from the possession of the person designed to be injured, or over whom some influence or advantage is to be gained, are thought most effacious. Such materials are usually wound up with thread, or placed in a vial or bottle, or gourd, words are muttered over it by the obeahman which converts it into an incantation. It is given to the applicant to take to the yard or path of the intended victim to be buried in the ground and this inanimate mass is believed to have the power of

---

[12] Ibid, Banbury p. 7.

[13] Ibid, Banbury, p. 9. See "Farmer death linked to obeah," **The Star**, Dec. 17, 1982.

[14] Ibid, Banbury, p 10. See "Vendors believe their money is being 'charmed away' by 'science men," **The Star**, Jan 7, 1983,
p. 7.

transferring itself in the body of the supposed victim without perception on his part, until he knows of its existence when he experience pain; and his only remedy is to have it 'pulled' out by another obeahman, if not the same one as sometimes happen.

"An obeahman can always 'pull' as well as 'put', 'Cure' as well as 'kill.' " [15]

All of this description of the obeahman/clients objectives/ends up as **"obeah" or "negromancy" /"necromancy" /"sorcery,"** which combines magic and superstition is best analyzed and described by Wodenoja's thesis, **Religion and Adaptation in Rural Jamaica**. He stated,

"Obeah is obviously an emotional and psycho-dynamic system as well as a cultural institution. It is cognitively based on an 'image of limited good' where it is assumed that one man's fall is another man's rise. Success brings fear of envy which in itself is believed to cause bad feelings." [16]

All of this he concludes gives the motive for obeah.[17]

There is, however, another objective motive, other than "success" which must be looked upon in relation to Africans being uprooted and carried into a new environment: the slave plantation, which had rigid concentration camp laws carried out by oppressive owners/masters/drivers etc. This point was noted by Banbury (in his above quote) when he stated, "*..the chief resort to the 'bushman' is to conjure either to kill outright or to afflict..."*

"Obeah," then, must be seen as a "psycho-cultural"/self preservation weapon against white and black oppressors: the plantation administration and its collaborators. Such would

---

[15] Ibid, Banbury, pp. 6-7.

[16] See W. Wedenoja, **Religion and Adaptation in rural Jamaica,** (University of California, San Diego unpublished thesis) 1978, p. 159.

[17] Ibid, Wedenoja, p. 161.

make the so called **"Obeahman"/ "Obeah"** - a positive functionaries in *the new plantation society,* to which he was forcibly implanted/acculturated to accept.

"The Obeahman": A Specialist, Medicine Man, Rainmaker, King and Priest from Africa

John S. Mbiti noted that in Africa,

> *"....magic is generally considered under 'good magic' and 'evil magic.'* ***The use of good magic is acceptable and esteemed by society.*** *It is chiefly* **the specialist** *and* **particularly medicine man, diviner and rain maker** *who use their knowledge and manipulation of this* **mystical power for the welfare of their community**. *It is used in the treatment of diseases, in counter-acting misfortunes and in working off or diluting, or destroying 'evil power' or witchcraft. The diviner or medicine man provide amounts of mystical powers to people in forms of charms, amulets, powders, rags, feathers, figures, special incantations or cuttings of the body.* **He uses it to protect** *homesteads, families, fields, cattle's and other properties."* [18] (my emphases.)

[18] See John S. Mbiti, **African religions and philosophy,** (Anchor Books Doubleday and Company Inc., Gordon City, New York), 1970, pp. 258-259. Note: the highlighting of certain words/sentences throughout this section is *the Author's* emphases, as it is these same **positive** traits/cultural action one will see in "Obeah."

These **"Specialists"** are by virtue of their specialized office, knowledge and skill in religious matters called **"Sacred Personage"/"Special Men."** They have suffered (as the Obeah-man on the plantation) from western-Euro-American writers/speakers and policy makers, who, too often and wrongly called them *'witch doctors'* (/*`obeahmen'*) - **"a term that should be buried and forgotten forever."** [19]

As Prof. Mbiti rightly described:

> "**In Africa the medicine man is 'a friend of the community.'** *There is no fixed role governing the 'calling' of someone to become a medicine man... In... cases a medicine man passes on the profession to his son or younger relatives. There are medicine men who believe there are spirits or the living dead have 'called' them...* **There are both men and women in this profession.** *Their personal qualities vary, but* **medicine men are expected to be trustworthy, upright morally, friendly, willing and ready to serve, able to discern people needs, and not be exorbitant in their charges.** *On the whole they have no official position outside their personal duties...* [20]
>
> *...They perform at seances intended to watch over, the witches, expose their intentions and frustrate their activities.* [21]
>
> *First and foremost, medicine men are concerned with sickness, disease and misfortune.*
>
> ...**the medicine man applies both physical and 'spiritual' (or psycho-logical) treatment**... *His medicines are made from plants, herbs, powder, bones, seeds, roots, juices, leaves, liquids, minerals... and in dealing with a patient he may apply massages, needles, or thorns and he may use incantations and ventriloquism, and he may ask the patient to perform special things.* [22]

---

[19] Op. cit, p. 218.

[20] Op. cit.

[21] Op. cit, p. 220.

[22] Op. cit, p. 221.

Another important duty of medicine men is to take preventative measures.... give aid to increase productivity,[23] *purge witches, detect sorcery, remove curses and* **control the spirit and living dead. They have access to the forces of nature and other forms of knowledge unknown or little known to the public.** *Therefore the public entrust them with the duty of removing what may harm the community.*

In short, the medicine man symbolises the hopes of society, hopes of good health, protection and security *from evil sources, prosperity and good fortune and ritual cleansing when harm or impurities have been contracted. These men and women are not fools...*[24]

These specialists have positive influence, with the collective community. *From time to time each community understands to smell or hunt the sorcerer and witches and punish them, 'cool' them off, cure them and counter their activities. Everyone.... keep constant guard."* [25] (my emphases.)

The acceptance of the **"Medicine Man"** as one of the. **"Specialist,"** in African tradition communities applies also to Rainmakers, Kings and Priests.

On the question of **"Priests,"** and clarity to a question which has baffled many Eurocentric minds: what is the separating line between "witchcraft" and "divination"? Summed up by Carlos H. Nelson:

"The diviner in the community is the consultant to verify these assumptions. So divination is not only limited to predicting the future but is also involved in determining what type of mystical angels are at work and who is responsible. Divination itself operating by mystical means

---

[23] Op. cit, p. 222.

[24] Op. cit, p. 223.

[25] Op. cit, p. 265.

selected from any possible agency. Therefore, it is reasonable to conjecture witchcraft and divination work together in presenting the total picture of the why of misfortunes." [26]

Thus these "Specialists" were "Priests" (Divinators /**Mystics**) and professionals likewise. All are inseparable in the Afrocentric cosmological perceptions. All these communal symbols/values/ interpretations became "fragmented" when Africans were uprooted by *'the triangle slave trade.'* These roles and arts remained, but only in a submerged form/**"masked,"** hundreds of years before *'white Christian orthodoxy'* was introduced upon slaves in these concentration camps: plantations.

---

[26] See Carlos C. A. Nelson, **Witchcraft (Explanation) divination..: a selected African project,** (African Caribbean. 1nstitute of Jamaica, 30.1.81), p. 5.

"Black Church"- "Obeah" in Revolt

One colonial account stated: [27]

> *"Prior' to 1655, Africans under the leadership of Juan De Bolas, a revolutionary African, engaged in a War of Liberation against the Spanish, using the hills in under-ground St Catherine as their base.*
>
> *When the English invaded in 1655 these African guerillas appear to have temporarily allied themselves with Spanish, who promised peace to them if the English was defeated. In 1655 the Spanish commander, Y. Sassi, who had been waging a guerrilla war in the hills, left Jamaica never to return.. Juan*

---

[27] See R. C. Ebanks, **The Maroon 1655 - 1740,** (A personal unpublished paper report) 1973-4? **Bro. Ebanks** gave this book to the *Author*, whom he thought is able to, literally further propagate the contents of this unique work; (at *the first University of the West Indies Afro-Caribbean Archaeological – Seville Project* - Columbus Beach Cottage, St. Anns Bay).

This Report is as a result of two journeys to Maroon communities: Accompong in the summer of 1973; Nanny Town in the winter of 1973. **It is the only one of its kind and is a "Historical Gem,"** which will be quoted from extensively. One should note keenly that Oral **sources** are used to verify historical data, made possible through the **living traditionally trained Specialists/Griots**, of these communities - respectively.

This work is particularly important, as it relates to Our first Ancestral Cultural Guerrillas, **the "Kenecuffes"**/The Pan-Black Maroon Front/Akan-Front. The point upon **the "Akan Front" (Coromantees and Madagascar)**/Pan-Black Front will be dealt with in our "Myal" section of this book.

See also Monica Schuler, **Alas Alas Kongo - A social history of indentured African immigration into Jamaica 1841-1865**, (The John Hopkins University Press Baltimore and London), 1980, pp. 33-4. She spoke of Akan ethnic secularism:

> *"...in Jamaica the Akan failed to recognised the inherent weakness of such national resistance in a heterogeneous slave population..." (p. 34).*

De Bolas fought on until De Bolas and a few others made peace with the English colonist and left the hills to dwell in the town. One section of the Maroons refused this - and instead settled in the remote and unexplored north east.

The second [account] is that when the Spanish fled the island in 1655, they left behind Y. Sassi who used the African people as guerilla fighters against the English . They held their own up to 1655 when the African leader Juan De Bolas defected to the English in return for the freedom of his people. Some Africans disagreed and returned to the north east. Whatever might have been the early beginning, the fact is that between 1650 and 1730, Maroons established a stable society in the north eastern part of the island. This society was based on African principles and traditions, a major cultural root being that of the Akan peoples.

In 1730 the Maroons had at least four major towns: Molly's Town, Diane Town and the great Negro Town... renamed after 1732 as Nanny's Town when at that time the Nya Nya established her war capital there.

Maroons were ruled by a woman called **Nya Nya**. *However, in peaceful time, day-to-day leadership was left to a captain or headman.* **The Nya Nya warrior leader chief, priestess and doctor assumed direct leadership during crisis**... [28]

---

[28] Op. cit, R. C. Ebanks, p. 7. Note the Nya Nya multi-dimensional rule, as versus the misperceived and imposed "secular" one-dimensional authority role. This should be further noted as the obeahman (and Maroons as well as other symbols, Black Churches and People) will be portrayed as multidimensional "Specialists" will. Upon this point, note the ideograph of E. K. Brathwaite, **"An evening with the status quo,"** (A Savacou Working Paper, Mona, UWI), 1982, p. 24. He noted,

> *"...from capsule core (religion/nam) the circle widens outward/back explode at time of crisis in response to dream or hope or vision... to all elements of the living culture held within a man.. priest becomes doctor becomes prophet becomes warrior becomes politics or statesman/diplomat becomes indeed*

The peace and security enjoyed by the Maroons up to 1729 resulted from the settlement patterns of English colonialism in Jamaica as dictated by the island's geography and colonial economy. Until then

---

the symbol of the nation, the ikon at the outer edge of the reality where ethics is aesthetics."

See also E. S. P. McPherson, **The Validity of Oral History as a Means of Historical Investigation: A Case Study of Rastafari,** (an unpublished Caribbean Studies, History Department, Mona, UWI, Jamaica), 1982, p. 94. Diagram Ill **Culture of Circle Man's Potential** (originally given to Author's class by Dr. [now Prof.] E. K. Brathwaite). See ideographs in E. K. Brathwaite, **"An Evening with the status quo,"** (A Savacou Working Paper, Mona, U. W. I.), 1982.

From 'Nam'/man-capsule core-to ikon

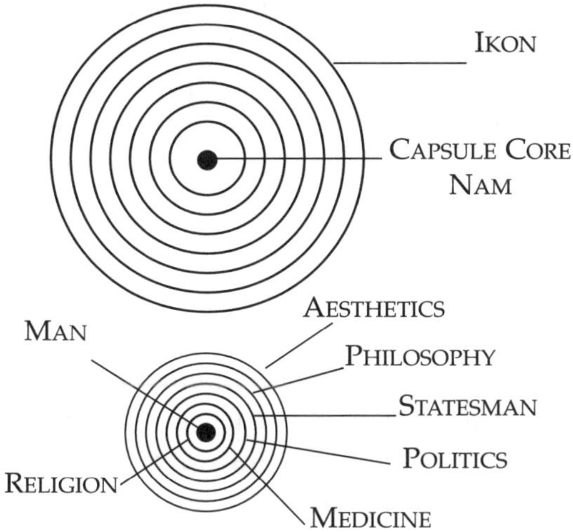

the major activity of the English had been illegal and 'legal' trade in goods and enslaved Africans within the Spanish whose port had been on the south coast. Before 1692 the trade had centered in Port Royal and after the earthquake of that year, in Kingston. Before 1731 all estates were centered in the most easily inhabited plain areas. The latter part of the 1720s saw the beginning of the final phase of colonial occupation of Jamaica. Under siege from Kojo and **the Kenecuffes** *in Clarendon, threatened by the Spanish from Cuba, and having a wealthy plantocracy which refused to fight or support any wars, the then Governor, Hunter, parceled out the largely unknown north eastern section of the island to any one who would settle in the island and do battle. Governor Hunter himself seems to have retained a sizeable estate for himself and enslaved Africans to work it. This began the Maroon War in 1728-1740 and* **the full emergence of the Maroons in Jamaican history***.)*[29]

In 1730 the title Maroon came to be applied to a group of African freedom fighters based at the time in the Clarendon and St Catherine hills. *This insurgent post was led by one Kojoe and had been established after an uprising in Clarendon in 1690.* [30]

...The Kenecuffes were joined periodically by other African people, **primarily those who had come from the 'Coromantees' coast***, and a group referred to as* **the Madagascar's***. Sometime before 1730 contact was made with the Maroon of the north east. This led to an alliance and a party of Maroon soldiers from the Cottage Wood section of the north east, who joined the Kenecuffes, Kojo retain-ing overall leadership in this central war zone.*

---

[29] Ibid, Ebanks p. 8.

[30] Op. cit, p. 9. This quote (footnote 20) is taken from Dallas, **History of the Maroons 1803 Vol. 1**, Letter 2, p. 34.

This war begun in 1690, could be regarded as the Kenecuffe or Kojo's war and the Maroon war of 1728 merges with it.

By 1730 the Kenecuffes had become, in effect, a government of black people in the bush and held sway over Clarendon and St. Catherine over such a section favored them while they apparently remained at peace on the plantation, **they exercised a dominion by the influence of obeah.** [31]

The word obeah is an English corruption *from the Akan word,* **obi**. It was *used by the English to denote any African religion which was uncorrupted by colonial culture. Thus the Kenecuffes had re-established a total African society complete with its religion and had come to represent to the enslaved people* **a free Africa and source of politico-religious authority**. [32]

---

[31] Op. cit, p. 9.

[32] Op. cit: Note Ebank's p. 2 of his Report - on obeah - is a critique upon **The Daily Gleaner** article of January 15, 1974, p. 1, ..,] giving the expedition members from *"'over the seas' view of their visits undertaken in the two Maroon localities." As Ebanks puts it, "...before leaving England the leaders of the expedition had built up* **a solid base of colonialist fiction by stating that they would defy Voo-doo on centuries old curses to carry out their mission**. *Upon returning to England they claim to having received death threats from members of the Maroon tribe"* (3) And that, *"a Maroon leader threaten the expedition with death by shotgun or cutlass unless they turn back" (4); and* **that, the expedition "defied a Voo-doo curse and death threat by tribesmen"** (5) And finally, *"all previous expeditions to this area have met disasters or accidents and the whole time we were distinctly ill at ease"* (6). (my emphases.)

Ebanks's after comment stated:

> *"Anyone who is acquainted with present day Maroon will know that* **they are neither 'tribesmen' nor 'Voo-doo' practitioners. <u>However, when using these words, it is important to note that in the language of the colonialist they have a different meaning than when used by black people.</u>** *Terms like 'tribesmen' and 'voo-doo' are* **used by racists to conjure up pictures of an ignorant so called uncivilised people... <u>Voodoo, like obeah, are manifestations of ancient African religious systems</u>. <u>The picture of these religions presented by the colonialist are pure fabrication</u>**..." (my emphases.)

In March of 1739 peace was made with the western Maroons and in June 1740, with the north eastern.

Events surrounding the signing of the peace treaty and the articles of these suggest that all was not well between the Maroons and Kenecuffes. [33]

As history recalls, the Maroons lived peaceably after this until the 1790s when these same articles began to be seen for what they were, tricks to deprive the Maroons of their hard won liberty." (my emphases.)

[33] Op. cit, p. 21.

'Black Church' in Revolt: Nanny - The Obeah Woman/ Rebel/ Queen/Mother 34

Figure 9: The Obeah Woman.: ***Rebel Queen Mother***

The authorities, had wrongly accepted a claim made in 1733 by Cuffee, *a very good party Negro*, that he had killed Nanny.

---

34 See Lucille Mathurin (illustrated by Dennis Ranstan), **The rebel woman in British West Indies during slavery,** (Africa-Caribbean Publication) 1975, pp. 34-7 Chp. 8 Nanny: Rebel/queen/mother. This **"historical gem,"** while giving a positive character profile/historical perspective of **"Queen Nanny"** speaks on magic"/"obeah" as it concerns **"Mother Nanny"**/ the Maroons, and is thus of relevance to this book/this section of the book - which portrays "Obeah" as a symbol of a "Black Church" in revolt.

Instead, she survived the first Maroon war and received on 5th August, 1740, her land patent duly granting, *"Nanny and the people now residing with her their heirs and assigns... 500 acres."*

Her legendary aggression and determination saw her pledging on the brow of Pumpkin Hill, in 1737, that, she and her people would continue to fight the English raiding parties to the death.

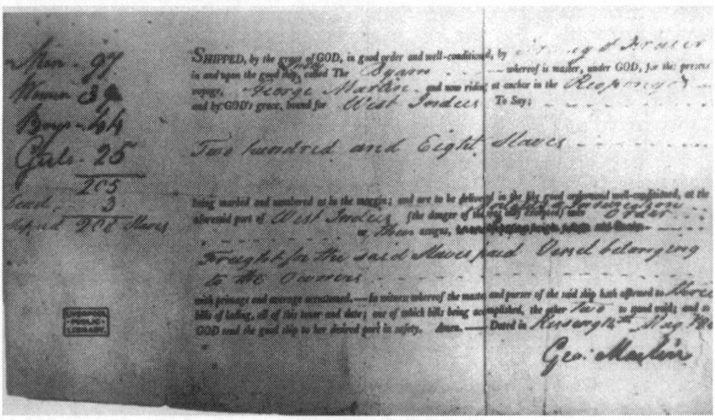
SHIPPED, by the grace of GOD, in good order and well-conditioned, by
Two hundred and Eight Slaves
Geo. Marlin

Figure 10: Document showing land grsnted to Shero Nya NyaNanny/The Maroons

She is said to have died in the 1750s. Her role is very much in the tradition of Ashanti Priest/Priestesses and Magicians who perform essential functions in African warfare.

These magico-religious leaders, ultimately advised on the best time for waging war; they gave warriors charms to protect them from injury. They participated with the Military Commanders in *rituals* designed to weaken the enemy.

Nanny became celebrated as a great worker of magic. In the words of a nineteenth century Maroon chief:

> "**Nanny had more science** *in fighting than even Cudjoe. After the signing of the treaty, Nanny said that* **she showed them science**. *She told fifty soldiers to load*

their guns and then to fire in her. She fold backwards between her legs and catch the fifty shots. This was called **nanatucompong**. *Nanny take her back to catch the balls."* [35] (my emphases.) [36]

'Black Church' in Revolt: 'General Tacky' - The Obeah-man/Priest 1760 Revolt

"In St Mary's pafh, a check was fortunately given at one estate by furprizing a famous obeish man or priefst, much respected among his countrymen. He was an old coromantin, who with others of his profeffion had been a chief in confeling and infligating the credulous herd, to whom therfe priefst adminftered a powder, which, being rubbed on their bodies was to make them in volnurable: they perfunded them into a belief that Tacky, their general liffinio in the woods could not poffibly be hurt by the white men so that he caught all the bullets fired at him in his hand and hurled them back with deftrictioll to its foes..." [37]

---

[35] Op. cit, p. 36. This fact is from oral source - a Maroon, and is a fact stated before in literate sources; but done so in a sarcastic way - Euro-biased way, as to denigrate **the Culture/Our Folk Culture/Popular Culture**. For a report of Tacky enactment of the NANATUCOMPONG, see Edward Long's, **History of Jamaica Vol.1**, (London, Jamaica), p. 457.

On p. 34 Mathurin stated: "Official documents give relatively scanty, but highly significant information about her (Nanny). It is recorded in **the Journal of the Jamaica House of Assembly** that she was, "**a obeah woman** *and that the largest and most formidable stronghold of the Portland Maroons were named after her."* [my emphases.] (This **Journal of the Jamaica House of Assembly** referred to must be, Vols. 111 and IV - see the bibliography of Mathurina, p. 41.)

[36] Op. cit, p. 36.

[37] Ibid, Long, **History of Jamaica, 3 vols.,** (London), 1987, p. 451.

The above quote is from Edward Long's, **The history of Jamaica 3 vols.**, (London), 1787, p. 451. It is the earliest West Indian document that speaks of the famous black liberator, **Tacky**, who was head of "the revolt" in 1760. This was a revolt said to have been organized by obeahmen, chief of whom was Tacky.

The above quote (which continues to p. 457 as well as in the other two volumes of Long's book) is full of glaring examples of Eurocentric bias/exclusivism/racism; but, should be accepted as the 'white' perception/"**the (old) Great Tradition"** [38] perspective of Our black culture struggles.

---

[38] See Edward Brathwaite, **The development of creole society in Jamaica, 1770-1820**, (University Press, Oxford), 1971, p. 230. He spoke of this "great tradition," thus

> *"...folk culture, though usually autochthonous, may be said to be dependent upon 'Great Tradition' in the sense defined by Redfield for it sanctions the memories, its myths. In the case of Jamaica slaves, the Great Tradition was claimed in Africa in the same way as white Jamaica was in Europe - both in other words external to the society."*

Note the footnote on the same p. 213, refers to, Robert Redfield, **Peasant society and culture**, (University of Chicago Press), 1936, pp. 41- 2. Redfield noted that,

> *"...in a civilization there is a great tradition of the reflected many. The great tradition is cultivated in schools and temples, and the little tradition works itself out and keep itself going in the lives of the unlettered in their villages/communities. The tradition of the philosophers, theologians and literary man is a tradition consciously cultivated and handed down. That of the little people is for the most part taken for granted and not submitted too much scrutiny or considered refinement and improved. The two traditions are interdependent..."*

Both quotes from Brathwaite have been given to define the differences between the great and little traditions. See also ibid, Mc Pherson, **The Validity of Oral History...**, p. 51. Long represents this so-called **"old"** tradition; a *school of thought* that has NOW been replaced by **"The Little Great Tradition."** Thus, *the unlettered people* (as *Myself*) could only interpret his quote (on p. 251) from a Black perspective. It portrayed the psycho-cultural patterns/forms that Our Foreparents - fighting Guerrillas - actualized. This we know, through literate sketches given by the Jamaican **"White Great Tradition"** scribes - as him. See Carl A. Lane, *"Concerning Jamaica 1760 slave rebellions,"* **Jamaica Journal**, Dec. 1973, Vol. 7 No. 4, pp. 2-4. Lane noted that *"in 1760 Long sat as a judge on Jamaica Vice Admiralty Court"*; Lane also concluded that Long was a *"pillar of Jamaican colonial life."* As we said,

Such a society clearly saw ***"obeh"/ "obeiahmen"*** as **A Priest/*"Priefst"***; seeing both inseparably. The embryonic plantation white society knew the obeahmen were "respected" among "their country men," "local Africans," "Coromantees." They saw the obeahman's role as a "profession" /*"profeffion"* and thus realized there was a set ordered hierarchy among them (and thus the mentioned *"caught victim"* /obeahman was seen as one of the "chief(s)" counseling/ "counfeling" and instigating/*"infligating" "africans"* /blacks described in racist terms as *"the credulous herd"*).

White society knew that part of their priestly/professional ritual was to have administer/*" adminftered" "a powder," "which being rubbed"* into the bodies of 'their slaves'/ these African, "was to make them invulnerable.'

There was a held belief among other obeahmen and black people about General/*"Genraliffino Tacky,"* of a powder which enabled him to catch bullets fired at him, which he hurled back at his foes.

Figure 11: The Obeah Man: "General" Tacky - 1760 Revolt

Long is to be seen as one from the **"Great [old] Tradition,"** who is thus Euro-biased.

What Long was here describing (though unknown to him and his white society) is the power of **"NANATUCOMPONG"**: *the Secret Ancestral Power*, which Nanny had actualized against white assault, during the first Maroon war.

From an *Afrocentric perspective*, **the "secret rite"** through which one was ordained with such **"power,"** does in fact make Tacky/all Obeahmen, priest/a *"priefst."*

It is **a "secret rite"** which *'white Christianity'* could not explain. (It MUST be here now noted that, as late as 1760, the white Christianity missionary assault had not even started - in full. Thus, for the first 150 years of the plantation formation/consolidation there was *'no God or Jesus, priest or missionary'* - on the plantation - within the lives of whites and, or, slaves - a point which will be expounded upon in another part of this book.)

By revealing that this *"caught victim"* /obeahman had been **a "Chief"**; and by the historical evidence of the systematic nature of this 1760 revolt, we have proof of the first "Inter-Communal-Revolt" [39] upon an embryonic plantation system

---

[39] Slave revolts can be classified in to three groups:

(1) individual acts of resistance which could be passive or physically aggressive;

(2) communal acts of resistance which are secularly centralized around certain communes/plantation/in one geographical area; and,

(3) inter-communal acts of resistance which were systematically co-ordinated between communes and was thus more widespread/effective.

Tacky's Revolt was organized among *the Obeah "fraternity"* throughout the island and had a inter-communal posture within it. The limited literate sources on this historically significant period validates the inter-communal nature of this revolt, and it's impact.

See C. Roy Reynolds, "Tacky and the great slave rebellion in the 1760s," **Jamaica Journal**, June 1972, Vol. 6 No. 2 pp. 5-8. He stated that this rebellion slated for Easter Monday night in St. Mary was, *"strategically chosen, as it was then sparsely populat-ed with whites and with deep woods."* With , *"fifty slaves mostly from Easter Frontier,"* there was march to Port Maria, that led to killings, the seizure of ammunition and guns, further leading to the plundering of White Hall, Heywood Hall, Esther and Ballards River. It invoked an emergence meeting of the Assem-

in Jamaica - and the Americas. (Note also, that the *"victim caught"* /obeahman was in St Mary, while on page 452 we find: *"...'Coromantins' and Captain Frurgts Estate in Westmoreland broke in rebellion"*; thus showing how wide-spread island-wide this revolt was.) It obviously rocked white society/the Jamaican plantation, as it was after this that laws were legislated against "obeah/obeahmen." And as Dr. [/Prof.] Brathwaite puts it:

> *"the ...obeahman... African trained or inspired..., men were almost entirely independent of white control and contributed enormously to the physical and psychological well-being of the slave population and therefore to the health of the society as a whole... A good obeahman will have influence throughout the district. These obeahmen (and women) received a great deal of attention from the white legislators, especially after the Tacky Slave Rebellion in 1760 which was said to have been inspired by them."* [40]

---

bly in September of 1760 which resulted in, *"mulattoes and free blacks"* being paid and used as *"bounty hunters"* of these slaves.

Reynolds further stated: This uprising was centered in St. Mary, Westmoreland while in St. Catherine, Tacky's plan called for an uprising at Luidas Valley, but three slaves pretended to take part in the revolt disclosed the plans to the overseer. Those who were not killed were deported to the slave penal colony in the Bay of Honduras.

Tacky's organization also covered plans for uprisings in St. Thomas, Clarendon, Kingston and St James.

In St. Thomas a slave named, ***Cuffy***, betrayed the rebels.

In Kingston, the band under the command of a ***'Queen of Kingston'*** were all deported. [See ibid, Lucille Mathurin, p. 21. The name of this queen was ***"Cubah."***]

Thus, the major uprisings were in St. Mary, Westmoreland and St James.

See also Carl A. Lane, "Concerning Jamaica's 1760 slave rebellions," **Jamaica Journal**, Dec. 1973, Vol. 7 No. 4, which disputes Tacky's responsibility for more serious revolt in Westmoreland, Manchioneal and Kingston. See also Ray Fremmer, "Trinity plantation and Tacky's Rebellion," **The Sunday Magazine**, Feb 24, 1985, p. 12.

For further reading upon the reasons for slave revolts in Jamaica, see E. K. Brathwaite, **"The rebellion in the Great River Valley of St James, 1831/32,"** (Mona, UWI), pp. 4-5. For further reading on the control of slaves see ibid, Mc Pherson, **The Validity...**, pp. 103-8.

[40] Ibid, Brathwaite, The **development of creole society**, p. 162; ibid, Long, p. 452; see **Jamaica Journal**, June 1972, Vol. 6 No. 2; see also ibid, Roy Reynolds, p. 7. Reynolds noted that :

This was an obvious response to the 1760 Tacky Revolt. Long said

> *"...The fame of General Tacky and the notion of his invulnerability ftill [still] [prevails] over the minds of others." (p. 452)*

Laws on "Obeah (/"Myal")

On the Ist of June, 1760 the Jamaican Assembly drafted a law against *"obeah - men and women"*:

> *"...and in order to prevent the many mischieves that may here after arise from the wicked act of negroes, going under the appellation of obeah men and women, pretending to have communication with the Devil and other evil spirits where by the weak and suspicious are deluded into a belief of their own having full power to... them, whilst under their Protection from any Evils that might otherwise happen; Be it therefore enacted... that from and after the First Day of June (1760), any negro of other Slaves, who shall pretend to any supernatural Power, and be detected in*

"...so great were the legislators' attention towards the obeahman that the House of Assembly 'forbade any gathering of slaves, decree that no slaves was to carry arms, that any slave leaving the estate ad to have a 'ticket', and that even overseers were prevented from leaving the estates on weekends or public holidays while free black, mullatoes and Indians had to register at the vestry of each parish and carry a certificate plus a badge showing their status.' Then there was the legislation against the practices of obeah, an 'official opinion seems to have been that the obeahman had played a vital part in the organization of the rebellion.' New taxation were levied on the people of Jamaica to offset the cost of upsetting the rebellion and to pay assisting conquerors. The British Crown in reaction to this revolt strengthened the military forces in Jamaica and many inhabitants were obliged to erect accommodations for troops in certain sections."

making use of any Blood, Feather, Parrot Beak, Dog Teeth, Alligator Teeth, Broken Bottle, Grave Dirt, Rum, Egg shells or any other materials relative to the practice of obeah or witchcraft, in order to delude and impose on the Minds of others, shall upon conviction thereof, before two Magistrates and three Freeholders suffer Death or transportation." [41]

This differs much in format and content from the later laws that were enacted against obeah. For example, with the rise of Myal, **the Obeah Law of 1898,** [42] read:

> *"Where as it is expedient to amend and consolidate the Law relating to Obeah and Myalism...*
>
> *3. In this law unless the context otherwise require 'Obeah' shall be deemed to be one and the same meaning as 'Myalism.'"*

Thus "Myal" and "Obeah" were seen through *'white spectacles'/the eyes of the plantocracy* to be one and the same by 1840. [43]

The later law carried a Euro-biased perspective/ interpretation of African cultural forms/symbols, as

---

[41] Op. cit, p. 162. It seems that the law against "obeah" became lenient in punishment as the years went on, as "death and transportation" were first the retribution upon the guilty ones of such an act; while in later days, lashes, imprisonment and fines were the punishment. See for example, **The obeah laws, 1898 in Jamaica Law 5 of 1898**, pp. 2-3. Note here (on p. 21) that lashes were stipulated for persons under age 16, above the age of 12 years, and under 12, implied that the practice of obeah was rife. It implied that this Black Church: Obeah - was embraced among the young.

This also was the same position for Myal, as the plantocracy 'laws' saw Obeah and Myal as one and the same.

Obeah had gathered strength, thus, ensuring it's longevity - evidenced by the distance of years between these legislation's, of 1760 and 1898.

Upon the law against obeah, see also, ibid, Leonard Barrett, **The sun and drum - African roots in Jamaica folk tradition**, pp. 73-5.

[42] Op. cit p. 1.

[43] Op. cit.

obeah/obeahmen and obeahwomen. In the 1760 legislation, his *"Pretending"* to have communication with the Devil and other evil spirits; *"...other slaves still pretend to any supernatural power"; "...practice of Obeah or witchcraft, in order to delude and impose on the minds of others...,"* are all not different from "a person practicing obeah." Meaning,

> *"...any person who to effect and fraudulent or unlawful purpose, for gain, or for the purpose of frightening any person.. ., causes or pretend to use any occult means, or pretends to possess any supernatural Power or knowledge"; "instrument of Obeah mean anything used or intended to be used by a person, and pretended by such person to be possessed by any occult or supernatural power."* [44]

Here for example, one cannot know what cultural value index/perspective, could determine a "pretender," or who had *"Supernatural Power"*/Knowledge; or who *"pretended"* to *"delude and impose on the minds of others."*

One could also see that the *"instrument of obeah"* (e. g., rags, feathers, blood, stone, glass etc. as stated in other parts of the law) can be found in and about the plantation environ, e. g., the huts of slaves/yards of slaves and masters etc. So, WHO then was to be the judge of them? Was it to be the collaborators of the plantation/plantation bureaucrats, the "Two Magistrates" or "Freeholder" to decide death or transportation? It certainly seemed so, as even later legislation gave more sophisticated plantation bureaucrats,

> *"...any officer of constabulary, constable, or Rural Policeman, (POWER) to arrest without warrant any persons practicing obeah."* [45]

Also too,

---

[44] Ibid, Brathwaite, p. 162.

[45] Ibid, Brathwaite, **The development..**, p. 3.

> *"..any person (who) shall compose, print, sell or distribute any pamphlet or printed material calculated to promote the superstition of obeah... such person (is) to be tried/if found guilty, [20 Pounds] or if in default to pay several months hard labour."* [46]

It is this vagueness that led Rev. Banbury to retail a case of an obeahman by the name of Shelly.

This case *"...was tried at Montego Bay many years ago, after confessing having employed obeah to inquiring people, he mentioned the fact of poisoning..."* The case *"proceedings were in the paper of that time."* [47]

Shelly *"was, dismissed on the plea of being mad."* This vagueness that was here exemplified by the obeahman Shelly, using madness as a rationale for his defense, led Banbury to conclude:

> *"The laws affecting the punishment of this superstition, in Jamaica are too lenient; otherwise it would not be so rife. The Courts of Justice are apt to laugh at the thing and treat it as a mere nonsense. But there can be no nonsense where people's life are endangered and actually taken away by poisoning, through the instrumentality of the Obeahman; so much mischief due beside amongst the people by setting them at variance with each other, at times causing dreadful assaults, even murder, as the records of the Courts of Justice will show."* [48]

Note however, previously, Banbury had stated in his introduction, *"..we are glad to find that the legislator has improved upon the punishment of the obeahman here at late."* [49]

---

[46] Op. cit.

[47] Ibid, Banbury, p. 9.

[48] Op. cit.

[49] Ibid, Banbury, (preface) p. iv; see also Errol Bowen, **"In Jamaica the occult lives and it's called obeah,"** Sept 9, 1973.

This same legal vagueness persisted up to the beginnings of the late twentieth century. It was combated in the said legal arena - of a post slavery and colonial based inherited courts:

> *"In one of his cases the late national hero N. W. Manley, Q.C., got a conviction in 'an Obeah case squashed back in 1933', when he successfully argued that obeah was committed 'according to the law, to the 'pretence' to invoke occult or Supernatural Power.' The case of the word "pretence" was, he supposed, because the formers of the statute did not believe there was any such thing."* [50]

Yes! the white plantation did not accept the existence of "Obeah" - genuine *ancestral specialists* - Obeah-Men and Women. The plantation did not see these *specialists* as ones who served *the People/Communities,* by **actualizing "works" for "the good of mankind"** (for animals plants: nature: the People: the Community: Nation and for/to the Afro-cosmos so much a part of the everyday doings of Africans/West Africans).

Failing to see such, the white man society/plantation colored the Obeahman as a ***"master grotesque and malicious"***: [51] **a *"sasabonsam."*** And this was so, especially after the 1760 *"Tacky Rebellion."*

These fabricated planter's laws were further challenged after 1760, as Long tells us, in *"July, 1760 several headmen of*

---

[50] Op. cit, E. Bowen.

[51] Ibid, Moorish, p. 44. Moorish gave a normative description of "obeah"/negative - obeah/"bad magic" (as Mbiti puts it) which links the Ashanti devil Sasabonson in such perspective of obeah. He said

> *"..a great deal of obeah ritual is concerned with this belief in duppies and the catching of a person's shadow by the 'shadow catcher' or obeahman. Because of its persistently anti-social activities, obeah gave rise to movements which sought to provide an antidote to its black and evil magic [as* ***Myalmen and women: Myalism*** *represents]. Obeah is essentially the worship of evil as formally represented by the Ashanti devil Sasabonson-Master, grotesque and malicious, associated with the woods and in particular the odum tree, which he uses as headquarters from which he captures unwary hunters. In conjunctions with the duppies the chief of demons give power to the obeahmen's fetishes."*

Coromantin met and conspired fresh insurrection... to take place immediately after Christmas." [52]

This plantation law could not stop the ever persistent and recurring "revolts," which were to come from "Black Churches," as "Obeah" - a symbol of the Black psycho-cultural/Black Spirituality cosmos in the New World. (Note **footnote 28** of this book.)

Yes! In the historic journey of the African Culture sojourning in *the west*, brought on by the evil of the "triangle-trade," which artificially imposed a plantation, **we** came up against white cultural aggression; and, **we** defended Ourselves through *"The Church": "Black Churches."* **We** were defended by **Obeah - Obeah Men and Women** as **Tacky** and **Nanny - the Maroons** and their predecessors: **the Kenecuffes**; and in later time **We** were further defended through **Myal**; **Kumina**; and *reinterpreted* ***'orthodox Christianity.'*** [53]

---

[52] Ibid, Long, p. 465 and pp. 473-75. At this point another Black Liberator and Obeahman (in the eyes of the authority and *The People/his People*) revolted. After the "black explosion" of 1760s period, **Jack Monsong/"Three Finger Jack"** emerged. His 1780-81 historical input ought to be noted. See L. Alan, "Jack Mansong Bloodshed or brotherhood," **Jamaica Journal**, Dec. 1973, Vol. 7 No. 4 pp. 9-14. Eyre noted:

> *"In the early part of 1780 the movement showed signs of growing into threatening revolt very similar indeed to the Mau Mau of Kenya. There was solemn oath taken, an African magical rites... Dr Benjamin Moseley, surgeon general to the Jamaican Militia, assistant judge for St. Andrew and a renown world authority on growing of sugar, mentioned a ceremony in which the contents of Jack's obeah horn were smeared on the forehead of his band to bind them to absolute secrecy."*

This book gives a good description of **Jack's/"Quashee's"/ John Neeler's/James Neeler's revolt** that began on the **10th Feb. 1780**, and his/it's - gruesome end.

[53] See ibid, Brathwaite, **"An evening with the status quo,"** p. 11a. This "psycho-cultural strength/Black Spirituality," as an organically created "alternative" to the white Jamaica plantation society illusion is best put by [Prof.] Brathwaite when he stated:

> *"Now there are two ways of approaching our sense of the alternative. One is superstructure. The other, is based on our own infrastructure. I don't only mean 'social system', 'economy', etc., but our entire psychocultural/ spiritual system where the strength lies."*

Such was not an *"accommodative" "response to slavery,"* [54] as *some* would have us believe.

The coming of "Christianity"

Up to this point, *"The basic grievance remained land hunger."* [55] And this, with other aspects of *the 'white apartheid policy'* of the plantation saw a symbol [56] of the Black Church, **the Maroons**, exploding in 1795-6, which came to be known **"the Second Maroon War."** The Maroons however lost (again), [57] and *"…were transported (man, woman and child to Novia Scotia), their town destroyed, their land confiscated and sold."* [58] Black opposition/ Black Church resistance was to now come through other means.

The *'missionizing'*/missionaries begun in 1754 when,

> *"...the Moravians were somewhat surprisingly invited by two wealthy plantation owners to send missionaries to their estate and they were the first Christian denomina-*

---

[54] Ibid, Wedenoja, p. 37.

[55] Ibid, Brathwaite, **The development...**, p. 250.

[56] Op. cit, pp. 248-50.

[57] Op. cit, pp. 248-50. Note, (again from the first war) such shows the Maroons had in fact

> *"..in 1740 after a ten years struggle against Britain/Jamaicans... being relegated and confined to the area of their high and rather barren reservation [p. 249], they were to be confined to slave catching."* [p. 249].

For readings on the fourteen articles of the treaties which. were signed, 1739 and 1740, see Beverley Cary, "The Windward Maroons after the peace treaty," **Jamaica Journal**, Dec. 1970, Vol. 4 No. 4 p. 19.

[58] Ibid, Brathwaite, **The development...**, pp. 250-1.

> *tion in Jamaica to attempt in any realistic way the task of teaching Christianity and its meaning to slaves."* [59]

The first of the **"five World Revolutions,"** [60] the American revolution, in 1776, saw fleeing loyalist starting the most significant missionizing beginnings - in the Baptist denomination. **George Liele/ Parson Liele** became the first **"Black Baptist"** in Jamaica [61] and he came in 1783, as well as others as **Moses Baker, George Gibbs, John Gilbert** etc., [62] These black missionaries became known as "Black Baptists."

Then, the Methodist came in 1789 [63] as also the Wesleyan Society [64] while Presbyterian came in 1827. [65]

Of all these "Christian churches," "the Black Church" was *visibly* symbolized most clearly by **the "Black Baptist"/"American Baptist" - "Free Slaves"** [66]. As a result,

> *"...the public leadership of a large mass of the slaves shifted from obeahmen to black preachers, evidence, cer-*

---

[59] Ibid, Moorish, p. 34; op. cit, Brathwaite, p. 252. For further reading on the Moravians in Jamaica, see Fred Linyard, **The Moravians in Jamaica from the beginning to emancipation, 1754-1838**, pp. 7-11. The Moravians were in the West Indies from 1732, in St Thomas.

[60] Ibid, Brathwaite, **"An Afternoon with the status quo...,"** pp. 10-18 subsection on **"World Revolutions"**; and pp. 11a-11b subsection on **"The American Revolution."**

The **five world revolutions** are: **the European Humanitarian Revolution** (from as early as) 1760; **the American Revolution** of 1776; **the French Revolution**, of 1789; **the Haitian Revolution**, of 1790; and **the Industrial Revolution** (that bloomed from the) mid 19th century.

[61] Ibid, Brathwaite, **The development...**, pp.163 and 260.

[62] Op. cit, p. 163.

[63] Ibid, Brathwaite, p. 35. He noted: *"The Wesleyan Missionary Society was founded in Jamaica, 1789 and its members were amongst some of the most enthusiastic in their desire to convert the negro slaves, and also to improve their physical condition and material environment and they quickly succeeded in arousing the anger and opposition of the planters."*

[64] Op. cit.

[65] Ibid, Moorish, p. 35. He noted that the Presbyterian Church of Jamaica was founded in 1824 and the Congregationalist followed soon after.

[66] Ibid, Brathwaite, **The development...**, p. 162.

tainly, of creolization ("inter-culturation") since it was now an element of the white man's religion that was being used by the slaves for their own spiritual purposes, though the extent to which the majority of slaves made any real distinction between obeahmen and black 'Christian' preachers, cannot be determined." [67] (my emphases.)

Despite **the 1793 Consolidation Slave Act** which, *"...had laid down that slaves were to be instructed in religion and baptism by their owners, the law was not widely observed.,"* [68] it was the same planter class whose, **"1808 Bill to prevent preaching by persons not duly qualified by law,"** [69] that came down on

"Black Preachers, who were not even 'always recognised as acceptable Christian Ministers by the white missionaries' [70] *e. g., Moses Baker, a Black Baptist was 'prohibited from Preaching under* **the Slave Preaching Act of 1806**.' [71] *'Thus like the obeah man this kind of negro was seen as a real threat by the white power structure and gave the Establishment considerable case for alarm'* [72] *e. g., John Gilbert, a Black Baptist Preacher was sent to Kingston work house for a two month sentence for* **'The Practice of this Black Itinerant** *among; the negroes and various properties to which he had introduced himself under pre-*

---

[67] Op. cit, pp. 162-3.

[68] Ibid, Moorish, p. 34.

[69] Ibid, Brathwaite, **The development...**, p. 260.

[70] Op. cit, p. 163.

[71] Ibid, Brathwaite, **The development...**, p. 163. The two different dates on **the "Slave Preaching Act,"** namely 1802 (p. 268) and 1806 (p. 163), has not yet been verified by *the author*. However, the rejection by the Privy Council refereed to: *"...the slave preaching bill of 1802 and 1807..."* (p. 10). The grounds on which the bill was rejected by Britain and the counter tactics of the Jamaican Assembly are noted on p. 261. (Of relatedness to this footnote, the Privy Council had, rejected "...**the Consolidated Slave Bill of 1808**." (Moorish instead gave the date as 1793, on p. 34.)

[72] Ibid, Brathwaite, **The Development...**, p. 163.

> *tence of instructing them in religious duties have occasioned much mischieves and given very serious case of alarm... that among pernicious doctrine he strenuously insisted on the necessity of the negroes fasting at least one day in the week... when... no work whatever either for themselves or owners should be done on Sabbath. The consequence of this was that the slaves particularly on one estate became from fasting spiritless, sick and emaciated, and being deprived of the produce of their own grounds... were driven to... plundering the property of their neighbors..."* [See E. K. Brathwaite, **The Development of Creole Society in Jamaica**, pp. 163-4.] (my emphases.)

One would have thought the so called *"Black Itinerant/"Pernicious Doctrine"* would have seen **"fasting"** as wholesome within *'white Christianity'* cosmology (as so many of **the Patriots** and **"The Christ"** *himself*, as too earlier Christians, even in Rome, dealt with such "Gnostic rituals"). This then should have been a part of *Africans/`slaves'* instruction into *"religion and baptism"* (as **the Consolidated Slave Act** empowered slave owners to see to).

Is it that "fasting," is different from 'baptism' and/`religion' when seen from a white Christian perspective?

One here also has to question the role of *"fasting"* in Maroon-Akan culture, as too in the Obeahman *"secret society."* [73] More so now, as many other black churches utilize this aspect of worship, e. g., as evidence through the oral and literate sources. One has seen **the Bedwardites** actualizing to the fullest extent this *Cosmic Mystery* of *"Fasting,"* as too, *"baptism"*;

---

[73] Ibid, Leonard Barrett, **The sun and the drum...**, p.70. He noted a most important point which will be taken on in a later part of this book on "secret societies":

> *"During slavery the legitimate priest and priestesses, unable to function in the slave setting, joined hands with the 'obeahman' to fight the witchcraft of the masters. They functioned as a secret society offering bullet, liquefying portions to the slaves performing ceremonial oaths, and administering herbal poisons to the enemy. These secret societies became strong institutions among the slaves, remaining unchallenged until the late 19th century when. missionary work began in earnest."*

and that, they too met similar resistance from the plantation authorities / post-colonial society, especially from the other Christian denominations.[74]

> *"The missionaries were... on the principle of their religious freedom alone in opposition to the white establishment because of this they were, by implication, on the side of the slaves. This appeared to be especially so of the Baptist."*[75]

Yet,

> *"..in general, however, the missionary societies were as colonial 'as the political society in which they had been given permission to function. To them their task was to pluck out root and branch, all vestiges of Eden (i. e., African) practices...' Above all obeah had to be confronted and defeated."*[76]

The radical revolutionary politics and "Liberation Theology" of the Obeahman / the Maroons, a "Maroonage" society - Black People - founded an "alternative" path to this *civilizing/ missionary/Christianizing* pursuit,[77] e. g. in the form of **"Daddy Deacons."**

---

[74] The Bedwardites laid an emphasis upon *"fasting and baptism"* in their form of worship.

[75] ibid, Brathwaite, **The development...**, p. 258.

[76] Op. cit, pp. 255-6.

[77] See E.S.P. McPherson, **"Brother Bedward" - A reason presented by E. S. P. McPherson, B.A. Hon. (U WI) at the Chapleton and District Historical Society Public meeting, Thursday 24th of May, 1984 7.00 p.m. at Salem United Church, Chapleton, Jamaica**, (Black International lyahbinghi Press, Frankfield P.O. Box 15, Clarendon, Jamaica), March 1985:

> *"By **'Maroonage'**, we mean that conscious retreat by the culture, away from the plantation (post-plantation) 'illusion' to the hills/swamps to build/establish A People Government/Community. Here, inward looking communal policies rooted in 'African Cosmology /Black Divinity': the Spiritual System: the psycho-cultural core of the culture - were applied to communal societal life. Maroonage saw to the question of 'food autonomy', defense (collectively) and governing based on gerentocratic principles. (1)*
>
> *One can also look at the concept of **'Maronage'** from even E. K. Brathwaite's,* **Contradictory omens cultural diversity and integration in the**

Firstly, ex-slaves and later slaves were permitted and encouraged to become 'missionaries' themselves. E. K. Brathwaite, writing on this embryonic formation of this stage of the development of "the Black Church" on the Jamaican plantations, said:

> *"So... the European gradually became conscious (conscience question) that they were doing an injustice to their human (other race). But what is more significant for overstanding of the development of the alternative, is that this conscience became so acute that they felt they had first to permit then encourage (black men, ex-slaves, later slaves) to themselves become missionaries (deacons, -conformist missionaries called them daddy's). The slaves came to call them because it was so much easier and so much more natural for black to speak to black and it conformed to 'rules of race': apartheid and its offshoot. And it was also plain good common sense. This is the thinking that permitted first Black Baptist, later the Black Deacons in the Christian churches. On this permission, permissiveness meant not only the possibility of conversion and the alternative it signified, but* **it meant legal assembly for large numbers of black people for the first time in the history of the plantation**. *Before that two was company and three was a threatening crowd. Now, during and after church, the slaves could talk of Christ, redemption and salvation from the sin of slavery.* **So plans and plots and preachments... as soon as Black Preachers/Deacons were allowed in Christ, they begun significantly to alter and erode the nature of their preaching from Euro-style to signify Christian, Afro-Christian, African.** *That was the continuum the preachers knew their*

Caribbean, page 58: *'...which holds/assumes that a specific cultural root or vision could come to be recognised as the norm and model for the whole.' (2)..."*

congregation wanted: from hymn to chant, from prayer to trump, from word to song to sound." [78] (my emphases.)

This resulted in what Prof. Brathwaite, rightly noted, *"Plans and plots and preachment"* manifested itself in this Black Church in 1831-2 revolt, popularly known as **"The Baptist War."** This was not due solely to the **"Native Black Baptists"** (as **"Daddy Deacon Sam Sharpe"**) as many literate works have depicted [79] but to the "Myalist/Myal."

As Monica Schuler puts it

"The Baptist War, referring to the so called Native or Black Baptist who led it and whose blend of African and European religious belief and practices was really Myalist and not Baptist." [80]

---

[78] Ibid, Brathwaite, **"An afternoon with the status quo,"** pp. 13-14a.

[79] See Edward Kamu Brathwaite, **"The rebellion in the Great River Valley of St James, 1831/32,"** (Mona, UWI), Feb. 1982. This book is the most descriptive account/analytic presentation of such a war.

[80] Ibid, Schuler, p. 34. Brathwaite's work quoted above, had noted that **Myal/Myalman "Hurlock"** input (and other Black Church elements combined together and are as such equally responsible for the emergence of this Revolt).

The etymology of "Myal"

F. C. Cassidy and R. B. Le Page, in their **"The Dictionary of Jamaican English,"** suggested that **"myal"** is of Hausa origins (**'maye'**) meaning 1. sorcerer, wizard, 2. intoxication, 3. return which are attributes in myal dance, man (and) woman. [81]

M. Schuler in her brilliant work, **Alas, Alas, Kongo, A social history of indentured African immigration into Jamaica 1841-1865**, contends the above origin of Myal's Hausa origins, saying, such is "most unlikely," and instead it may be Central African. However, Central African descendants in St. Thomas parish, members of the Kumina religion (see Schuler, Chp. 5) describe powerful spirit possession as ***"catching myal."*** [82]

She, however, warned that,

> *"…from its inception in Jamaica myalism does not seem to have been associated with any specific ethnic groups and*

---

[81] Ibid, F. C. Cassidy and R. B. Le Page, p. 313.

[82] Ibid, Schuler, p. 136, footnote 8. Kumina, as a Black Church, and its relations to Obeah - will be later looked into. See Schuler's **Chapter 5**, for a description of kumina - "spirit possession" - seen as myal. See **"Imogene Kennedy, an informant (taped in Trench Town, Kingston, 24th May, 1971),"** p. 76a:

> "'When we get myal we can find a thing bury (that is, an obeah charm), but when we normal we can't do these things', while on p. 78, she speaks 'on the violent manifestation of 'spirit possession' when the myal going take you now, you whole body becomes like you cold. See and you see you feet them draw and you neck... sometime you neck fall away back ya so... myal is the thing they call a spirit where you head spin round and you drop, and you skin proper (puppa) lick pon you neck, you see? That a myal spirit. That's mbongo myal spirit which all the old African them, them come round and them lick you all on your head side and rise you pon your neck and you drop. You see? That there mean to say, myal hold you now.'"

was probably a blend of west and central African belief and practices." [83]

Myal: "The Myal Man"

Monica Schuler noted that the planter - historian Edward Long, the first European to record the existence of myal religion, referred to it in the 1760s as *"a new society open to all."* Its initiation ritual, which he called *"myal dance," "provided invulnerability to death caused by Europeans."* [84] According to Long,

---

[83] Ibid, Schuler, pp. 136. Such a point is related to the already mentioned Pan-African character of Myal, as versus, the ethnic organizational secularity - as a front - against the plantation (ibid, Schuler, pp. 33-4.) Akan centered uprisings/ cultural groupings ."..fail to recognise the inherent weakness of such national" resistance in a heterogeneous slave population..." (pp. 33-34.)

In our footnote 27 we noted that in the first Maroon war, Kenecuffes, Coromantins, Madagascans and Akan ethnic groups came into one solidified front thus showing that at such an early stage, Akan people did realise "the inherent weakness of such national resistance in a heterogeneous slave population." Demographically aware of such "heterogenousness" (of the slave population) **must** have dawned upon the Akan people. Demographically, Akan - were not the majority. See Ken Post, **Arise Ye Starvelings - The Jamaica Labour Rebellion of 1938 and its aftermath**, p. 155 footnote 90. Post noted, "in the opinion of Williams, the Ashanti may undoubtedly be declared the dominant influence in evolving our Jamaican peasant of the present day (Ibiden 142). We may add that this may not be because of numbers since most slaves exported from the former Gold Coast were not Akan, Ga and Adangme, Guang-speaking peoples and others like the Dagomba, Mamprussi from even north" were also taken. (See Orlando Patterson, **Sociology of slavery**, pp. 119-22, 135 and 137-9). Post concluded rightly: "The whole subject requires much further study." There were other Pan Black Front revolts as in 1798 and 1831/32, which we have already mentioned (along with Schuler, p. 34).

[84] Ibid, F. C. Cassidy and R. B. Le Page, p. 313 for myal dance description which is reprint from, ibid E. Long, p. 416:

> "Not long ago since, some of these execrable wretches (obeahmen) introduce what they called the myal dance and establish a kind of soci-

"...candidates enacted a ritual of death and rebirth in the myal dance by drinking a mixture of cold water and rebalbroched calalu and then dancing until they reach a state of dissociation resembling death.

The application of another mixture revive the candidate."

85

---

ety in which they invited all they could. They lured frank out was that every negro initiated into the myal society would be invulnerable from the white man and although they might in appearance be slave, the obeahman could, at his pleasure, restore the body to life. The method by which this trick was carried on was by an infusion of the herb branch calalu which after the agitation of dancing threw the party in a profound sleep. In this he continued to all appearances lifeless... till on being rubbed by another infusion (as yet unknown to the whites), the effects of the calalu gradually went off, the body resume its motion, and the party, on whom the experiment have been tried, awoke from a trance, entirely ignorant of anything that had passed since he left off dancing. This herb is a species of socamum... The myal gentry make the infusion with rum in regard to the other infusion which puts an end to its operation, we can only conjecture."

For a further account of myal dance, see, M. G. Lewis, **Journal of a West Indian proprietor, 1815-1817**, (reprint in Britain and New York, Haughton Mufflon Company), 1927 pp. 354-5.

In Cassidy and Le Page, **Jamaica Talk...**, they defined/described the myal dance as, *"a dance performed under the effect of 'spirit possession' in the African cult and similar one."* (p. 313.) (my emphases.)

[85] Ibid, Schuler, p. 32 refer to the calalu plant which is "a member of the solanaceae family, West Indian spinach, apparently narcotic when soaked, un-cooked, in cold water."

Figure 12: Myal Myalman Hurlock & 'Daddy Deacon' Sam Sharpe "The Black Baptist-Myalist War" 1832/9

E. Long's Eurocentric report, the first in **the "Great Tradition"** archive/literate world, is most instructive to this book. This myal dance, an African religious tradition/, *"spirit possession" dance*, is seen by Long as a *"trick"/"experiment"* been tried, was carried out by *"obeahmen," "execrable wretches."* His *"conjectures"/"the unknown to the whites"* - did not/ (/could not) know/interpret this Obeahman/Myalist Cosmology. Evidence of this, led to "Myal" being described/seen as a form of **"witchcraft,"** and not clearly distinguished from **"Obeah."** [86]

"Myal"/a king of a society," was thus seen by white plantocracy as a (continuing) opposition as - "obeah." Thus we find by the beginning of the nineteenth century, "obeah and myalism" are equated as the same: *"...obeah shall be deemed to be of one and the same meaning as myal."* [87]

---

[86] Ibid, Cassidy and Le Page, p. 313.

[87] Ibid, A quote from/in **Jamaica Law 5 of 1898,The Obeah Law 1898**.

The perspective on the **Obeahman and woman**/Obeah has already been given. The differences between **the "Myal-man/woman": Myal** from **"Obeah - obeahmen,"** can be gathered from their respective cosmologies. This was made more possibly, especially at the point of later days Myalist - at the beginning of the 19th century.

At this time Christianity missionizing was well on its way and the Christian dogma had penetrated the Myalist Cosmology, e. g., Myalist retorted,

> *"...we cannot keep peace till Jesus tell us to keep it. The Spirit is all over the world; the myal task they preached was to clean the land for Jesus Christ who was coming among them... Clearing the land for Jesus Christ meant eradicating the obeah through special public rituals which only myalist could perform."* [88]

Myalism was different from "Obeah," but in *the author's* view (as well as others like M. Schuler), ***it was Obeah in a re-vitalized/ masked form***. As M. Schuler noted:

> *"...a movement may even seen to disappear when in fact political hostility has only driven it underground to re-emerge, as myalism did repeatedly, under more favorable condition."* [89]

---

[88] Ibid, Schuler, p. 41 and note, p. 36: "Myalist extracted and emphasised two central themes of the Baptist faith: The inspiration of the Holy Spirit and Baptism, in the manner of John The Baptist, by immersion because they seem to correspond with belief or symbols already familiar to them." (This is another example of Christian dogma infused in a later resurgence of myal.)

[89] Ibid, Schuler, pp. 33. For further study of "Millenarian movements," read Klaus de Albuquerque, **Millenarian movements and the politics of liberation: The Rastafarians of Jamaica**, (Virginia Polytechnic Institute and State University, 1977, pp. .37-131. In this work there is a scientific demonstration of the "revitalization"/"routinization" theory, as a structural and socio-psycho-dynamic cultural mechanism of a "Millenarian movement." In this book: **From "THE BLACK CHURCHES..."** the development and process of **"Obeah"/ Myalism**, represents such "revivatlization" movement(s).

The original crux of myalism cosmology asserts that

> *"...under ideal circumstances good prevail absolutely and exclusively, but in a real world of limited resources, where such perfection really exists, anyone employing unusual good fortune is suspected of doing so at the community's expense. Such anti-social people, placing personal goals above those of the community are thought to employ ritual to satisfy their self-centered desires, they practice magic or sorcery, harnessing the malevolent forces believed to permeate the universe and produce evil. The major function of religious rituals which, unlike magic, is always community centered, thus become the prevention of misfortune caused by the anti-social and the involvement of the community's good fortune."*

This presented world oriented tradition refused/refuses to accept as natural dissension, poverty, corruption, illness, failure, oppression:

> *"..all the negative disappointing tragic experiences of life. Believing that sorcery caused these evils, this religious tradition claims to possess weapons with which to eradicate them, an arsenal that includes not merely ritual techniques, but constant assertion of community values, positive responses to social change and maintenance of social order."* [90]

So the Myal/*"mial people"* who are

> *"...persons favored with communication from the 'spirits' 'fo-yeyed' (four eyed), that is, they can see spirits and conversed with them...',* [91] *were 'grasping the evil... and destroying it', in all respect for the good of the community."*

---

[90] Ibid, Schuler, p. 33.

[91] Ibid, Banbury, p. 19.

"Maye," meant **"evil,"** and **"le"** meant, **"to take hold of, to grasp."** This meant Myalism **"see"** and **"grasp the evil."** [92]

Myal then, was not, "...excitement bordering on madness" as Russell said. [93] Myalism functioned to explain/predict, and control the people into a continuing dynamic of African tradition. [94]

Myal/Obeah and ("Black Baptist"/) Christian orthodoxy

From the first report of the *"myal dance"* given by E. Long, the line of distinguishing between myalman and obeahman has been debatable among historians. This book has reflected on this subject in a previous section.

There is the view by F. C. Cassidy, in his **Jamaica Talk**, that *"...the obeah-man had already made myalism a part of their practice and corrupted it."* But how can one be sure of such when, both Obeah and Myal (in their earliest arising) were *"secret societies"/"secret activities"*? This is one of the reasons

---

[92] Ibid, Moorish, pp. 45-46.

[93] Ibid, Cassidy and Le Page, p. 313; ibid, Russell 1864, p. 6.

[94] Ibid, Schuler, p. 33. Schuler's footnote 10 pays tribute to Robert Haughton, "African conversion," **Africa**, Volume 41, 1971, pp. 96-7. She stated: "Haughton's emphasis on the importance of the Three Fold Functions of explanation, prediction and control is reinforced by a quote in Moore, 'Religion', p. 178, where a kumina adherent explains that he avoids the Roman Catholic Church because after conversion the priest 'gives no explanation and no knowledge.'"

why contemporary observers sometimes confuse them. In Ken Post words, for example:

> *"Obeah was witchcraft, the manipulation of the spirit world by specially skilled, usually for the purpose of harming others. By its very nature, therefore, it was a secret activity. [And yet] Father Williams argued that Myalism was in fact the practice of traditional Akan religion, its priest oppose to obeah but also forced to work secretly, because under slavery all African religious practices were forbidden. This would help to explain the undoubted links between them which causes contemporary observers to confuse them."* [95]

Ivor Moorish, also, gave a view of Myal being a "practice of traditional religion":

> *"Myalism appears to have been the old tribal religion of the Ashanti in which the Supreme Being Nyame Nyankonpon was worshipped and there was also veneration for the minor deities (Aboson) subordinate to Nyamkompon, who appeared in Jamaica in the guise of the Accompong."* [96]

This African traditional form, he continued,

> *"...openly oppose the obeah-man and was in part almost fanatical in his zeal to destroy the works of the evil obeah, and he demanded a fetish oath of allegiance from initiates in his Myal society...."* [97]

---

[95] Ibid, K. Post, **Arise Ye...**, p. 141.

[96] Ibid, Schuler, p. 46.

[97] Op. cit, Father Williams in an extract from the Boston Evening Transcript, Jan 7 entitled, **"Catholic priest alleges local devil worshipping,"** said: "Jamaica reeks with obeah from end to end, black magic, traced centuries by to African fetish and idolatry." He distinguished between obeah and myal and declared them to be religious:

These two Black Churches cultural forms are closely related. It appears that from

> *"...the beginning there was an exchange of function between the obeahman and the myal man. (But as some writers noted:) The same individuals, who performed obeah (called 'black magic' by the Europeans and called 'white magic' by the Myalist) rites at night would undo his own work the following day... The dualism with obeah is preserved, in that today, the obeah-man is often to offset bad obeah. That is, he may obeah or bewitch a person but is amenable to persuasion by gifts or otherwise to remove the obeah."* [98]

What was to cause a further "dualism" in the theological and societal perceptions, were these two Black Churches, Obeah and Myal inter-culturation - synthesis - with 'orthodox Christianity.' It was a "religious/cultural" synthesis, from which came **"Afro-Christians"- "Creoles"** (i. e. those with "altered consciousness" who became "alternatives"). [99] In this *"masked" personality,* a cultural weapon in the form of **"pre-emptive parallelism"**[100] was created by the enslaved popula-

---

> "...voodoo, myalism, obeah, each is inexplicable. Each began as a religion but all have decayed into devil worship... myalism was originally the religious practice of the tribe whereas obeah was formal witchcraft... Myalism... has been antagonistic to obeah, though many who have spent a lifetime in Jamaica are inclined to confuse the two. The obeahman works through fear and seeks the harm of the individual."

[98] See Fernando Henriques, **Jamaica**, Chapter 10, **Cult groups**, p. 186, pp. 184-195.

[99] Ibid, Brathwaite, **"An evening...,** pp. 19-23 in a section called the Mind Maroons, the neo-mask, disguise of man (alternative, he stated: **"...he can disguise the soul, planted in human soul, can alternate... he can reverse by consciousness so it remains, remains un/dumb protected and submerged."** (my emphases.)

[100] See Madziwanyikas Tsommdo, "Against alienism: The response of desireness and apostolic independence - Christian church movements to European colonialism in Zimbabwe," [pp. 201-319.] p. 297, in David Channaaiwa (edited), **Profile**

tion, and was last seen in *the "Baptist-Myal War."* This went on through out the 'given' 1834/38 apprenticeship period.

This Afro-Christian racial consciousness grew in strength. It resulted in the natural reaction of the plantation: repression!

Even Afro cultural forms/arts as **"John Conoe"/"Konnu"** [101] was forbidden, in Kingston, 1841. This resulted in *"...a riot which the police could not control and the military killed two men in restoring order..."* [102]

The Afro-Christian cultural assault by "Myal" and this Black Church penetration upon 'orthodox Christianity' resulted in/revealed itself by 1841, when the *"Baptist association had split over the infiltration of African religious practices into local chapels."* [103] *"Native Baptist(ism) grew in strength, white sponsored version dwindled."*

It was in St James and Trelawny - the center of Myalism in the 1820s, 1830s and early 1840s that Myal, an Afro-Christian symbol "revived" itself. Myal kept resurging/submerging and again resurging more widespread, *"in 1841-2, 1846, 1848, 1857 (in Kingston itself) and 1860."* [104]

> *"The Myal movement begun in December 1841 and lasted until repression drove it underground in November*

---

of self determination - African responses to European colonialism in southern Africa (California State University Foundation, Northridge, 1976. He stated:

> "Prophetism combats Westernism with pre-emptive parallelism which means the former's acceptance of the concepts of the latter's culture but in order to effect them in a manner that appears so 'advanced' as to dwarf and denigrate the latter. This goes hand in hand with 'reverse parallelism' - a counter-culture upon the aggression/ acculturation assault of the oppressor."

[101] See Sylvia Wynter, "John Konnu in Jamaica," **Jamaica Journal**, June 1970; ibid, Moorish, pp. 64-6.

[102] Ibid, Post, **Arise Ye...**, p. 142.

[103] Op. cit, Post, pp. 142-3. See Philip Curtain, **Two Jamaica...**, pp. 164 and 169.

[104] Ibid, Post, p. 143, ibid, Curtain, p. 170.

of the following year (1842)... It began in Spring Estate in the St James coast about six miles from Montego Bay and eventually affected some twenty-two plantation villages.

Since 1838 a number of unexpected deaths had occurred in the Spring Estate Village; these were ascribed to obeah, which was then blamed for every misfortunate. During Christmas of 1841 tenants of Spring invited Myalist from near by Ironshore Estate to spring clean of obeah and everyone but the Presbyterians in the villages participated in the ceremonies." [105]

The Myal revival arose through out St James, into Trelawny and Westmoreland, and as far as St Thomas in the Vale by 1842. [106] The Myal movement apart from absorbing/reinterpreting western Christianity, visibly unmasked itself, to appear and function as an ordered Black Church: *"There were in the 1840s three grades of membership: archangels, angels and ministering angels."* [107]

Here, one has to distinguish between the **"Mind Maroon"** conscious alternative - the **"masked"** African Black Church, - and the full **"creole" - "Num,"** [108] i. e. a non-person; whose is **Nam's/Man's opposite**. M. Schuler stated that

"...on occasion elderly Africans were accused of practicing obeah. Africans were already part of the aging section of the population in St James in 1825 and at that time lived either in elementary families or as... solitaries with solitary jobs... If this pattern of social isolation of older Africans persisted into the early 1840s, it might well explain their becoming objects of creole suspicion. Since many myalists

---

[105] Ibid, Schuler, pp. 40-1.

[106] Op. cit, p. 41.

[107] Op. cit.

[108] Ibid, Brathwaite, **An evening...**, p. 37.

were young men... [note the laws against obeah/myalism evidently by then had been directed at the young as already stated in this book). In a parish that had suffered an increase in male mortality rate for over a decade, fears of death and suspicion about the secret of African longevity might have influenced these accusations. Such accusations might also have stemmed from creole fears of job competition from new African arrivals, with whom the old Africans had expected to join.

On at least one occasion creole accused African captives of obeah. Such accusation led to a riot on Running Gut Estate in St James. The privileged position of lighter skinned creole also attracted myalist attention. In non-cultural areas like St James, colour and status were the most clearly related, resulting in a great revival attention."

Thus Myalism/Myal-Obeah links still persisted amidst the creole and white perceptions of the plantation. This also qualifies the classification of **"Afro-Christian"** as being more "Afrocentrically Christian," than 'Christian orthodoxy.' It qualified these **"Cultural Guerrillas"** as **"Mind Maroons,"** who *consciously masked*, and collectively combated the planters and missionary acculturation strategies

"Myal wrath 'was directed against planters and missionaries'; it intended /utilized industrial action'/political worker revolt action, e. g., in 1842 when a 'planter... summon the police to stop the performance of myal ritual in their estate' which ended in an attack upon the constables, arrests, the burning down of the police station and (most importantly) the denouncing of the authorities 'beginning with the Queen and proceeding downward to the Governor and local magistrates'; [109] *it was abusive/ aggressive to Christian orthodoxy interference, e. g., when Rev. Hope M. Waddel, a Presbyterian with many parishioners... tried, to*

[109] Ibid, Schuler, p. 42.

break up the myal ritual on Blue Hole by accusing female myalists of madness, members turned on him in anger, stating 'they were not mad, they have spirit. You must be mad yourself. You had best go away....'"

Myalist persistently tried to gain new converts from out of the missionaries' organization/membership.

So the Myal movement (obeah in the eyes of many),

"..in 1841-50 years after this Baptist word was first preached on the North Coast. Myalist offered something more hopeful, quite simply the millennium." [110]

"Several measures taken by the authorities against myalist temporarily checked its public manifestation. Within three years the ritual was performed again on Trelawny Estate and it continued to be observed throughout the 1850s. In the 1860s, it became the basis of another regeneration movement..."

Thus, as Monica Schuler quite rightly summed up:

"Jamaican planters perpetuated the very affliction myalism had been designed to counteract. They understood correctly that Myalism threatened that control." [111]

"As it moves off the plantation, myalism stimulated in its members sentiments of unity which transcended the divisions in Jamaican society, sentiments reasserted in the Great Revival of the early 1860s."

The Myal tradition forms the core of a strong self-confident counter-culture. It guaranteed that none of the evil of past slavery period would be accepted passively but would be fought ritually and publicly. This inevitable lead to periodic confrontation with the island authorities or any group consid-

---

[110] Op. cit.

[111] Op. cit.

ered to be perpetrators of misfortunes or destroyers of harmony. Myal People were a symbol of an Independent People Black Church.

It was in this atmosphere of "cultural solidarity/Pan African co-operation," that Myal persisted in strength from the 1840s visibly/publicly revealing and resurging itself, that the West Indian Immigration Scheme was conceived by an *beaten alien-plantation*.

The coming of Africans from Central Africa further ignited the Black Churches, and further confused the plantation - missionaries - creoles' theological perception of Afro-religious cultural forms. [112]

Kumina/Cumina arose *in the east*, St Thomas, and this Central African veneration of *the Ancestors* further threatened Western Euro-Christian ("professed") monotheism.

The etymology of "Kumina"

The etymology of the word **Cumina** (with its variants such as **Kumina, Kumona, Krumuna, Koominah, Cummona, Crumuna**) is not clear.

F. C. Cassidy and Le Page suggested that two or more words of related meaning are probably combined. The Twi word, **"kom,"** connote **"'to dance widely in a state of frenzy or ecstasy,"** ascribed by natives to the agency of a fetish **"nkommoa," "spirit of possession."** The Kimbundu word,

[112] See for example, of obeah, myal, kumina, inter-relatedness/ usage interchangeable (as viewed by the plantation, in, ibid, Wedenoja, pp. 39-40. He noted myalism was "by the planter as but a dance" and therefore tolerated for entertainment. It contained elements of kumina and developed into the cult of myalism which grew out of obeah and the slave revolts." (p. 40.)

"kumona," means **"to see,"** [113] **("implying that under possession by the see ancestral spirit the participants are endowed with the power to see the world of the occult and to have paranormal experiences'").** [114]

It was *a dance/ceremony in memory for the departed,* in/through which The People/tribe individually and collectively became possessed while dancing and evoking the spirit. It was a religious dance held on nine nights, births, betrothals, memorials etc.

Ivor Moorish noted another possible origin of Cumina /Kumina:

> *"There is another African cult word used in Jamaica namely, cumana, which has reference to 'calling dead' mother. Although this is not related etymologically to Cumina it, nevertheless, refers to similar rituals in which the spirits of the dead are invoked. It is just possible that there is some connection between the Jamaican practice and some of the ceremonies of the aboriginal Arakawa Indians for apparently cumana is a term found in the Arawak, Venezuelan region of South America."*

"Kumina" – "Obeah"/"Myal"

It was Dr. E. K. Brathwaite who beautifully stated:

"Kumina is basically a circular religion, conceptually in terms of the life spirit stream and more physically a lifestyle of a community. By means of a spirit possession a person becomes a god and

---

[113] Ibid, Moorish, p. 59; ibid, Cassidy and Le Page, p. 267.

[114] Op. cit, p. 52.

communicates freely with the ancestor god and descendant gods who are yet to be born. As a mediator a possessed person sends a message to the mundane world. Invocations and provocations (called obeah) possibly especially by the fast rhythmical drumming and dancing (and whole/music) which leads to an ecstasy over the sacred." [115]

Figure 13: Kumina: The Spirit of Africans Survival Arising

[115] See Yoshiko Shibata, **Rastafari music in Jamaica, its historical cultural significance of socio-religious music in culturalogy of area studies**, (University of Tsukuba, Japan) Jan 1981, pp. 14-3.

Kumina is a new world Bokongo "survival":

"Kumina is to put it more accurately, the living fragment of an African (mainly) kongo/religion in the Caribbean/ Jamaica. It is a fragment because the slave/plantation system did not allow more than fragments: the visible public aspects of the incoming (so-called 'deracinated').

Africans were, in the instructive interest of control suppressed; the social language, the social hierarchies, the specialists, the public observances and therefore the officials of symbol, regalia and publicly expressed ritual, link and memory were destroyed. Therefore African culture in the slave world, kumina, had to survive and it had to survive as long as the people who lived/ expressed it survived, had to submerge itself, had to lose much of its public visibility, had as it submerged, to accept losses, to adapt, miraculously, creatively did this, persisted and survived, which is not as surprising as it first sounds, and would not be so at all if we stopped thinking of kumina (religion) in terms of European medieval definitions of it: church, pope, ecclesia, and conceive of kumina (and religion generally) once more as an aspect or focus of culture so that worship is seen as a particular kind of social observance based on faith/assumptions but not in any permanent separated from other more 'secular' customs. Indeed, we must begin to think of a situation where the word/concept sacred and secular are practically meaningless or rather where they connote a certain kind of intensification of a shared organic experience." [116]

"Kumina is an original Congolese religion/culture having an ancestral teacher, an elder/`the old African(s) Tatambenza/Mbenze/old man or the tree of the Ngunza queen priestess' [117] *who expresses such a survival cultural form.*

---

[116] See E. K. Brathwaite, "Kumina - The spirit of African survival," **Jamaica Journal**, No. 42, p. 46.

[117] Op. cit, p. 47.

He/she expands 'atomically' to be priest/priestess, politician, economist etc., through the power of Nommo, spirit force and meaning of the word. It is (they 'who remember and restore the past')." [118]

Kumina is basically African and non-Christian.

To many - as the *author* - **kumina is the most African of the earliest un-masked Black Churches in Jamaica.** Meaning, it has negligible European, or (Euro-western) Christian influences. (This/these views are however open to challenge.) The Christ influence upon/in Myal has already been seen in this book, but what of Obeah?

Obeah, was veiled with a similar "secrecy," as stated before is a "secret society/fraternity." Did Obeah take on this 'Christian' outlook?

Yes! would be the answer, if one accepts that Myal was Obeah in a resurged form. We however see them as two separate Black Churches - respectively.

Upon Kumina and its origins, the same veil of "secrecy" exists:

"There are varying theories as to whether it was brought with late African arrivals after emancipation or whether it was rooted in Jamaica from the 18th century (or before) and deepened by the later African influences." [119]

Kumina is found primarily in St. Thomas and to a lesser extent in Portland and St. Mary.[120] To a reasonable extent, the religion of Central Africa in St Thomas in the east remain the religion of the microcosm, the source from which Central Af-

---

[118] Op. cit; ibid, Schuler, p. 73: *"Greatly respected queens are 'scientist' like their myal counterparts - counselors, doctors and ministers to the people."*

[119] See the section called "kumina," **Jamaica Journal**, Vol. 10 No. 1, p. 6.

[120] Op. cit.

ricans securely stayed, although they did participate in Jamaican society over more than one hundred years. Thus, as Monica Schuler said so potently - almost from the beginning of her seminal work

> *"...central Africans had one foot in the 'African world' and the other in Jamaica world, although as long as they live primarily in their own communities the greater part of their religious life was liked to be focused on the cult of spirits of recently deceased Ancestors, 'min kuya', the shades."* [121]

The Kuminaist was also **A Diviner/Healer** as the Myalist and Obeahmen and Women; and they shared with Myalist, *"the significance of memorial ritual for the dead (and) belief in a dual soul."* [122] In both dance/ *"spirit possession,"* it enabled *"the evil to be found"* . And like Obeah(men) it had power of invocations or provocations. This was said to be: **"Pulling" - protecting from "putting."**

However,

> *"During the immigration period of the 1850s Africanist Diviners were still looked down upon by white and creole plantation societies, e. g., a Presbyterian teacher George Gordon expelled sixty Africans from his Broomsville Church Settlement fearing 'that some of his class were secretly patronising the scientist..'."* [123]

Yet, the Baptists *"made the most inroad upon these Africans"*; [124] many became converts/ **"Baptist,"**

---

[121] Ibid, Schuler, p. 71.

[122] Op. cit, p. 72.

[123] Op. cit, p. 85.

[124] Op. cit, p. 86.

"..these conversions and the ultimatums against African rituals and African scientist fail to eradicate them... Moreover apart from some obvious material benefits (e. g. literary) offered by conversion... most African in Jamaica, like Africans elsewhere and like earlier myalist, could derive the desired benefits from Christianity without really converting, that is, by merely adopting familiar elements that parallel their own beliefs. Thus the missionary version of African 'conversion' was, essentially inaccurate." [125]

The Black Churches Obeah, Myal, Cumina, Black Baptists (and other Afro-Christian Black Churches) were to further arise more visibly in strength, against a professed "white" 'monotheistic orthodox-Christianity.' There arose **"Revivalism."**

Both Cumina and Revival rituals had thus reflected, and no doubt fostered unity with Central African and creoles, developed out of necessity over the years. They symbolized the way in which the African immigrants accommodated the new Jamaican society/"masked" themselves in the Jamaica society. [126]

Revivalists too, were to be seen in the eyes of *'the authority'* and other *'orthodox Christians'* as "obeah." [127]

---

[125] Op. cit.

[126] Op. cit, p. 47.

[127] Cumina was first mentioned in literate sources 1943; Cumina lingua - language: Kikongo, is the least corrupted of the "Black Churches":

"Both Yoruba and central African descendants have strong tradition of old arrivants' attempts to keep African customs, including languages from the prying eyes and ears of creoles and other outsiders." (ibid, Schuler, p. 182.)

Revivalism: Puku and Zion – its etymology and connections with Obeah/Myal and Christian orthodoxy

"The Baptist had lost financial and numerical support in the late post emancipation period and with only a small recovery of membership in the 1850s as versus the heyday of the 1840s, a recruiting campaign had been decided upon in February 1860 and revival meetings had been held in western parts of the island. Until November, however, the response not being encouraging and when the great movement actually began in Manchester (February)... It was joyously hailed by the missionary bodies, the revival for which we and minister and churches have been so long praying and labouring has at length been realised in the numerous districts and islands."

As the first Revivalist took to the road, they were joined by others along the way. [128] Thus,

"..what came to be called the 'Baptist Revival' began among the Moravians in the Manchester parish and spread to the former denominations (thus the Baptist joined with Moravians, [129] *which was planning a revival movement."* [130]

[128] See Douglas, Hall, **A Free Jamaica 1838-1865 An economic history**, (Caribbean Press), 1959, p. 238.

[129] See Edward Seaga, "Revival cults in Jamaica - Notes towards a sociology of religion," (reprinted from **Jamaica Journal** Vol. 3 No. 2, June 1969, pp. 3-4.) He noted "the Baptist joined with the Moravians who had in the past being very exclusive and other non-conformist churches to form the backbone of the movement."

[130] Ibid, Post, **Arise Ye...**, p. 143.

"The means of achieving salvation implicit in the Great Revival were far more African than European. These stemmed from the myal (from the 1840s to 5Os) and going even further back, from the basic African religious belief that the spirit world was not separate and apart from the temporal but from one unified whole.. ." [131]

Figure 14: Revival- in motion.

As the Great Revival, however,

"..subsided in 1861 but, reappeared in 1866 in the wake of the Morant Bay tragedy ('Morant War') of the late 1865, the revivalist soon left behind the missionaries who frowned in disapproval of myalist or African practices such as dancing, drumming and spirit possession - evidence that the Great Revival had more in common with myalism and

---

[131] Ibid, Seaga, p 4.

> *African revitalization movements than with Christian revivalism."* [132]

Only accident, it would seem, dictated that the movement began with the missionary fold. The Myal tradition would have been sufficient inspiration but it is likely that African immigrants religions (Kumina being one) which belong to the tradition, after all, also contributed some elements to the revival. [133]

Many religious sects which exist in Jamaica today possibly owe their existence to the Great Revival. Cumina is thought to have given birth to "Puku" - so called *'pocomania'* - and Afro-Christian sects which have spread beyond the boundaries of St Thomas in the east. The movement of **Pastor Tate** of **the Abeokuta Yoruba**; from **the Baptist**, to **the Holiness Church** may have taken place at this time. At any rate Abeokuta was reportedly one of many Westmoreland countries devoted to what one official in Jamaica condemned as, *"...the excessive and extravagances of the persons called themselves revivalist."* [134]

What is most important here is the speculation of **Cumina** giving birth to **Puku**. One writer stated:

> *"Pukkumania began in the 1920s and to him in general term was a revival of the magical beliefs and trance techniques of African religion blended at the more emotional and ecstatic levels with Christianity....."* [135]

The first literate reference to "pukkumerian" (Puku) was in 1929 (see Beckwith, pp. 176-7):

---

[132] During the 1850s myal received a upsurge, myal was cloaked/ "masked" in "Christian revivalism" and was called *"Methodist revivalism,"* ibid, Post, p. 142.

[133] Ibid, Schuler, p. 104.

[134] Op. cit.

[135] Ibid, Moorish, p. 52.

> *"Revivalist and obeahmen unit in the particular religious cult known as the pukkumerian. The name is used in derision, says the followers of this cult for they are really revivalist like the rest..."* [136]

Revivalism/Puku's birth, however, was from the mid 1860s (in *the author's* view) and as Schuler said,

> *"The bonds between revivalist held as strong and tightly in 1866 as they had with myalist in 1840s."* [137] *In fact, a Professor F. Henriques traces its origin back to the myal movements of the slaves which were directed against the obeahman."* [138]

The etymology of Puku points to the Myal origins. The Twi word, **"po,"** means **"to shake or tremble," "kom"** means **"to dance in wild state of frenzy,"** and to these two elements it is possible that Myal has been added, thus making this (Black Church) a 'cult' (in the eyes of *the system)* - which mingled revivalism with ancestor spirit possession. [139]

Another suggestive, and the reason for the author's **"Puku"** or a **"Pukkumina"** spelling is that the Spanish word, **"pocomania,"** saw **"poco"** meaning **"little"** and **"mania"** meant **"madness."** Thus implying that the practitioners were a **"little mad" ("little madness")**. But, as "there is no evidence of the Spanish linkage or derivation," one can only see it

> *"..more closely linked semantically with cumina, surviving as a previously African religious cult which absorbs*

---

[136] Ibid, Cassidy and Le Page, p. 356, ibid, Seaga, p. 5. Note - a finite similar twentieth century classification stated:

> *"In addition, the census had used the term pocomania referring to pukumina to which many persons could not admit membership classifying themselves somewhat euphemistically as 'revivalist.' This is especially true of pukkumania members who mainly used this term in reference of themselves. Zioness on the other hand are not as particular and will accept membership as Zioness are revivalist."*

[137] Ibid, Schuler, p. 104.

[138] Ibid, Moorish, p. 52.

[139] Op. cit.

> *myalism and became permanent in the second half of the last century. After introduction it is said by post emancipation African immigrants to St Thomas area in the 1850s..."* [140]

Thus, some what like Myal and Kumina, the Revival movement withstood the Jamaican society hostile reactions to such West African and Central African polytheism. In effect, a Pan-Black Church Front organically developed. And as Schuler noted:

> *"...left to themselves then, Africans express no hostility towards Christians, and members of separatists. Afro-Christian sects were not hostile towards Christians. Moore, for instance, found a cordial expression of cumina and revival fellowship in their attendance to each others fellowship. Revival spirit respect and enjoy cumina, know the Gods of the Africans, but do not dance... Cumina followers come to revival, love the Holy Spirit, but do not dance."* [141]

The same Afro-Jamaican unity/West African-Central African unity came under attack in 1865, and resulted in many

> *"Africans who took no part in Bogle's struggle (he was a freeholder, they were not; he was a Black Baptist Daddy Deacon Christian, they were not) nevertheless they were treated as rebels, flogged and even executed and thus they displayed certain ambivalence towards Bogle."* [142]

---

[140] Ibid, Seaga, p. 4; ibid, Cassidy and Le Page noted 1943, Gleaner, Kingston:
"Pocomania, a religious cult... puca...co-myal, a kind of headan [heathen]. worshipping; called poccomeea, a legion's mania; while 1950 G. Moore, p. 6 stated that: Pocomania, also called Poco - 'The black Israelites' looked upon with disfavor by all the other cult groups who consider it devil worship.. ."

See also Ferdinand Henriques, **Jamaica**, p. 87: Pocotiempo which means *"of no account"*; ibid K. Post, p. 156 footnote 107, M. Beckwith, Puku Ke, i. e., *"Tick them here"* and *"Die here for the buried obeah."*

[141] Ibid, Schuler, p 87.

[142] Op. cit, p. 107; and for a further see for example, pp. 108-9.

Upon "revivalism"/revivalists," **"Zion"** as versus **"Puku"**; and, upon how they relate to Obeah, [143] note:

(i) In Zion spirits usually do not reside at the 'ground' because the Zion pantheon give far less recognition to human spirits, and more to the heavenly or biblical host. [p. 6 as versus Zion deal with 'ground' spirits constantly, these are considered evil by Zion cult..." (p. 13) and (pp. 10-11 called 'fallen angels'];

(ii) Pukumania regard Zioness as more experienced in matters of healing (p. 13). Healing and obeah are two of the principal forms of magico religion Behaviour... (p.11) forms of attention given are (1) social and (2) psychological through 'readings' and here Zion and puku primary areas of association is on matters of healing and obeah;

(iii) There is very little magical behavior. That is, behavior that is not explainable in terms of spirit influence. Magical beliefs are terms science by revivalist and the source of supply of this belief is invariably one of the numerous books published by De Laurence Company of Chicago, U.S.A. For example: **The Great Book of Magic and Art/6 and 7, 8 and 9 and 10 Books of Moses, Hindu magic and Indian occultism**. All banned under **the Banned Publication Act, 1943**;

(iv) Puku possession at the outset is 'usually experience by a paralytic shock in one leg followed by a recession of consciousness. The individual stomps the other feet at the moment of seizure and falls forward as versus, Zion possession pattern is usually not abrupt in its onset. Groaning usually proceeds the possession...(p.7) Zion spirit possession... usually last no more than one to three hours;

(v) There is far less significance of obeah among pukus (p.12);

(vi) Law does not forbid revivalist groups but they sometimes infringe **the Night House Prevention Law of 1911** and

---

[143] Ibid, Seaga's article is best for this comparison.

the Obeah Law of 1908 (and the **Banned Publication Act of 1943**);

(vii) Despite their many fundamental the public sometimes are made aware of their ritual meetings but there are those that are unadvertised/secretly organized (p. 13)"

Thus, from the speculated beginnings of "Revival" 1850 - mid 60s, to the literate declared,

> *"Redeemers came forth from the wilderness in the latter part of the 1880s stimulating the growth of revivalism when in 1886 a woman began to hold street meetings in various parishes."*

Early literate source also further declared that a certain,

> *"..brand of revivalist recently discovered her in a cave in a forest where she lived since 1860 and Angel had fed her daily with locust and honey."* [144]

This revolutionary tradition grew in strength [145] - that by the 1980s *The Revival Movement* was to get *official recogni-*

---

[144] See W. F. Elkins, **Street Preacher, Faith Healer and Herb Doctor in Jamaica, 1890-1925**, (Revisionist Press, New York), 1977 p. 3. See also **The Daily Gleaner**, Nov. 3, 1987.

[145] Ibid, Schuler, p. 105:

"The voice of revival because it partook of the myal tradition could also be revolutionary. In 1865 it spoke through the warning of a 'son of Africa' posted on the Wharf Gate in Lucea Hanover: 'I heard a voice speaking to me in the year 1864 saying "Tell the Sons and Daughters of Africa - that a Great Deliverance will take place for them from the Hand of the Oppression; for the said Voice, they are oppressed by Government, by Magistrate, by Proprietor and by Merchants. And this voice says: "Tell them to call a solemn assembly... and the sword would come from America. If the people depend upon their alms and upon our Queen and forget Him who is our God they will be greatly mistaken and the mistake will lead to a great distress." '

"But great will be the deliverance of the Sons and Daughters of Africa - and the children of Alawah... If we pray truly from our hearts and humble ourselves we have no need to fear. If not... they will be gog and magog."

tion/support from the head bureaucrat, **the** [then] **Prime Minister Edward Seaga**.

This recognition, however, was **a "culture brooking" act** (to use one of **Hoetink's** socio-cultural classification)! For example, the [then] P. M. [Seaga] is an Anglican (and a Lodge member). The general lay public, however, is left to ritually continually query (annually) if "Revival" is to be seen as demonic? (i. e. is 'obeah'). Or, was "Revival" to be seen as a genuine Afro-Christian denomination of orthodox Christianity - a post-plantation 'professed monotheism'? [146]

---

[146] Upon the 1980s *'revival debate'*, this will be spoken of more extensively in **"Book Two"**; for now, read the latter original section from which this work, **BOOK ONE**, is derived: E. S. P. Mc Pherson, **From "THE BLACK CHURCHES" To THE NYAHBINGHI ORDER: THE YOUTH BLACK FAITH**, (A H350 History Department, Mona, UWI, lecture presentation project), May 1983, p. 160, pp. 206-7, footnote 79i, pp. 207-8, footnote 801.

For this **footnote 79i:** *the author* regrets that the dates of these articles can not be given due to reprinting errors: Read, "Obeah is ancient African religious rite, Burnham," The **Daily Gleaner**; "Paper raps Guyana's bid to legalise obeah," **Sunday Express** (Port of Spain, Trinidad), Nov. 4; Mitzie Clarke, (Student, UWI), "Counteract his onslaught of Satan!" **Daily News** (Letter to the Editor Feedback), Nov 25, 1982; Margaret Morris, "Watt Town Revival Schoolroom," **The Sunday Gleaner Magazine**, Nov. 21, 1982, pp. 1-3; Laura Tanner, "Kumina: The Kongo connection," **The Sunday Gleaner Magazine**, Dec. 5, 1982, p. 1; Rev Ernie Gordon, 5 Cower Dr., Kingston 20, "Revivalism, kumina, a Christianity," **Daily News** (Letter to the Editor) (Feedback), Oct. 26, 1982; "Philip St John Hill, Priest explains Zion revivalism ('moving into the spirit is our most precious facility' in Religion," **Daily News**, Sun, April 17, 1983, p. 6; Billy Hall, "Revivalism yet again!" **The Sunday, Daily Gleaner** (Church Commentary), p. 16; Arthur Kitchin, "Our national heritage," **The Daily Gleaner**, Oct 11, 1982, pp. 8-17; Arthur Kitchen, "Rituals and spirits," **The Daily Gleaner**, Oct. 25, 1982, p. 8; John Hearne, "Revival and the church," **The Daily Gleaner**, Oct 28, 1982, p. 6; H. A. Brooks (Mrs.), 6 Bramwell Dr., Kingston 8, Oct 19, 1982, "Revivalism," **The Daily Gleaner** (Letter to the Editor) Oct 29, 1982; Billy Hall, "Roots of cults," **The Sunday Gleaner** (Church Commentary), November 7, 1982, pp. 8, 19; Rev. B. L. McLeavy, Moravians Church, Betharbara Newport, Manchester, Oct. 29, 1982, "Revival and Church, **Sunday Gleaner** (letter to editor), Oct. 29, 1982, p. 18.

On a regional (i. e. Caribbean) level see also**"...but the church is skeptical,"** (Reuters, Georgetown), Nov. 9; Alister Hughes, **"Legalising obeah,"** (St. George's, Grenada); **"Forbes Burnham defends obeah decision,"** (Georgetown, Guyana), No. 7; Ulric mentus, "Catholic versus pro-obeahist," **Caribbean Commentary**, p. 22; Carl Wint, "Can obeah ever be made respectable," **Daily News** (Nation's business) (Kingston Jamaica); Slave Pickney, "The matter of obeah," **Daily News** (Let-

Many churches arose through the 1860/61/65 revival, such as **Convince/Convince Doctors** in the 1890s that

> *"...claimed they are able to cure disease with 'blessed water, interpret all mysteries, counter obeah effects and secure evil spells. They told the people that God had raised them up as prophets and doctors for good of the oppressed negroes of the island to deliver them from slavery and oppression of the white doctors and parsons.'* [147] *Revivalist balm yards, Church of God, Pentecostal and Four Square arose from this Great Revival also."* [148]

It was, however, the continuing Native Baptist "Black Baptist" Uprising of **Wood's** and **Bedward's Jamaica Native Baptist Free Church** (JNBFC) which continued to link "race" with "revivalist" revision, wrapped into an outcry against poverty, [149] that continued the march of the Black Churches.

---

ter to the editor Feedback); H. P. Jacobs, **"First in two part series - Obeah, culture and colonialism"**; Trevor Adams, **"Obeah makes a come back,"** (Bridgetown, Barbados - Reuters).

[147] Ibid, W. F. Elkins, p. 4.

[148] Ibid, Elkins, pp. 2-4: "During the late 1770s and early 1880s **Stewart Haddo, 'Doctor'**, had thousands visiting his balm/ healing encampment which he later gave up. He used drums and sang Salvation Army choruses." (ibid, Mc Pherson, **"Brother Bedward,"** (March 1984), p. 1. Upon "Balm," see the most detailed study done by Joseph K. Long, **Jamaica Folk Medicine**, (Ph.D., Dept. of Anthropology, University of California), 1973; ibid, Mc Pherson, **The Validity...**, pp. 114-5.

[149] Ibid, Ken Post, p. 143.

Revival - The Native Baptist/Black Baptist Church in Continuing Revolt: Shakespeare/Bedward Fasting vs. Pernicious doctrine; baptism/balm/healing vs. Water craze/superstition

H. E. S. Shakespeare Woods came from America at an early date, not positively known, and lived in Spanish Town whence he was called by God to live in St David in about 1876. He was very peculiar: he lived in a stone hole or cave in the wilderness from whence he habitually came on missions of love, to preach the word of God and prophesy. In June 1879, he visited Dallas Castle, St Andrew and prophesied that there would be a destruction by a flood. This in fact came on the 11th October, 1879. It destroyed a Wesleyan Chapel, among other buildings/ properties, and took several lives.

In December 1888, he visited August Town and prophesied a similar destruction for August Town unless the people repent. He gave *"order"* then for a general meeting of the then three existing denominations in August Town, Anglican, Baptist and Wesleyan to hold *"a solemn Feast unto the Lord."* Only Baptist and Wesleyan obeyed and a number of people assembled on the 19th April 1889 on Papine Pastures. Shakespeare said: *"The Lord is coming and will soon be here."*

Then there was the sound of a strong wind, followed by a light drizzling rain and then a remarkable and general prostration (as on the day of Pentecost). All were filled with the spirit. 43

After then, Shakespeare withdrew into an apartment where there was a large jug of water from the Mona River. Upon the jar a *Bible* was placed and he called in by name twelve men and twelve women constituting them into twenty-four elders. Each one at a time laying his or her hand on *The Bible* while expressing the solemn vow to be faithfully devoted to the service of God even unto death. It was on this occasion that he declared:

> *"There is one among you who shall succeed me and be leader of a Great Religious Movement which shall be centered in August Town and it shall be a blessing to millions. As yet, however, I know not who he, my successor, is."*

After the election of the twenty-four elders, he elected two chief men, Robert Ruderford, Baptist and Joss Walters, a Wesleyan, to see to the observance of a monthly fast in this congregation. The observances were kept up by them over three years. Shakespeare further prophesied among them in this period:

> *"..that a fountain will be opened in August Town, but the man to rule it was not yet ready."*

Shakespeare changed his residence from St. Davids to Spanish Town in 1889 and paid occasional visits to August Town to see how the work prospered. He lived till age 101 years, and was buried on 20th March, 1901.[150]

On the 19th April,1889, Alexander Bedward stood among the 24 elders and heard the prophetic remark, *"one of you shall succeed me...."* He had no idea that it would be him.

Bedward was born of very humble parentage in St Andrew, Jamaica in about the year 1859 and was remarkably and uniquely prepared for the prophetic work.

He was severely sick for 13 years and after consulting many doctors he resorted to a change of climate and went to

---

[150] See **A. A. Brooks, History of Bedwardism or the Jamaica Native Baptist Free Church, Union Camp, August Town, St. Andrew, Jamaica, B.W.I.**, (Jamaica the Gleaner Company Ltd., printers, Kingston), 1917,pp. 2-4; ibid E.S.P. Mc Pherson, **The validity...**, section called **Black Churches, Shakespeare to Bedward to Roman 1880-1930 ('St. John' 'De African Griot') to 1980s The Ethiopianist thrust**, pp.114-126.

Colon, Panama in 1883. He stayed there for two years and regained his health but on returning to Jamaica in August 1885 he was immediately seized with the old disease. He thus left the following Saturday returning to Colon.

On his 6th night of arrival in Colon he had two remarkable visions the last of which ordered him to Jamaica

> *"I do send you to August Town. Go to August Town, submit yourself to Mr. Ruderford for instruction with fasting on Mondays, Wednesdays and Fridays, then be baptised for I have special work for you to do."*

This Bedward did though reluctantly. He left Colon; arrived in Jamaica on the 10th August, 1885; and was baptised by Mr. Ruderford the second Sunday in January 1886.

Figure 15: Black Baptist "Brother Bedward": Fasting Baptism & Healing at The Hope River.

He worked on Mona Estate for five years, up to the 10th October, 1891 and on that day he was specially called by God for some clarification and thus. commenced his public performance at the Mona River dispensing the water as medicine and baptizing.

Bedward received *special revelation* concerning the potency of the Mona water and on the occasion of his first fast on December 22, 1891 there were about two hundred sick persons of whom however only seven would take the water as medicine and they were immediately cured. They henceforth devoted themselves to the tri-weekly fast in the Baptist Church. [151]

The news of the potency of the water having gone forth, from far and near, afflicted ones would come and many are the cases that never came in vain. A general excitement was created. The civil attention and hostility were aroused.

In June 1893, the government tested the waters of Mona River. The island chemist, John Bowrie, test proved (though it was not made public or was it put on any government record) "that it contained every medicinal property excepting castor oil." [152]

August Town became a "balm"/healing to the nation(s) using the professed monotheist orthodox Christian doctrine in a "pre-emptive parallel style":

> *"New things are always looked upon with suspicion, but a curative agent the August Town medicine has no equal. Thousands of people are to be seen on both sides of the Hope River on Wednesdays. And Mr. Bedward, conductor, uses*

---

[151] Ibid, A. A., Brooks, pp. 4-6, pp. 12-13 for tri-weekly fasting procedure.

[152] Op. cit, p. 6; ibid, E.S.P. Mc Pherson, **The Validity...**, p. 116: From **Oral Sources**:

> "**John:** ...Bedward gave three years for water... medicine to bring in the crowd. Three years and the whole world send and check the medicine... You were saying some Americans come and checked it and found all the medicine in the world... except castor oil. And after the water gather a crowd, den now the first baptism. At the end of three years the work begin."

no other weapon but the bible and praise and prayer... The water tell for itself from the wonderful cure." [153]

Bro. Bedward/the Bedwardites "Black Itinerant"/ [154] "Fasting and praying and baptism" [155]was not/never supported by the *'established church'*: "the Anglican/'Church of England'" as seen from the inception of the **J.N.B.F.C. - The Jamaica Native Baptist Free Church - The Bedwardites religion**. Shakespeare *"had called a solemn fast unto the Lord"/"a general meeting of the existing denominations in August Town,"* and they - *'the church of England'* - alone - did not turn up.

This **"balming center"**/*"Black Itinerant"* was classified as *"superstitious"* and was also attacked by another branch of *"the Established Church."* Bishop Gordon, head of the Catholic Church in Jamaica, **"in a notice to all Catholics in Jamaica**

---

[153] See **"Ministering to the Bedward craze - correspondence Copy of an extract composed by Mr. A. Grant, teacher of Cedar Valley School, St Thomas."**

[154] Ibid, Brathwaite, **The development...**, pp. 163-4. We have already noted the value system of the British and Jamaican plantocracy *"Old Great Tradition."* Such a school-of-thought, in the nineteen century, saw **John Gilbert**, a Black Baptist, in a negative manner; and did the same, from 1890-1921, to **Bro. Bedward**, a Black Baptist/ **the JNBFC**, whom they also saw in a negative manner. John Gilbert ministry, that included "fasting," was purported by the plantation to make slaves "among other things, 'spiritless.'"

[155] Ibid, Schuler, p. 86:

> "Moore had discovered in his research that kumina/central Africa felt especially close to Baptist and revival because they baptise in the river and are close to the river gods come around a great deal to protect them... That it is a protection from evil spirit or 'bad wind.'.. protection against abduction by spirits of the dead or by spirits that have never been human..."

Although the Bedwardites did not direct their theology to a pantheon of gods, one has to also note that the Bedwardites had emerged after the revival carrying with it the same West African/Central African people who still had the concepts as those of *"baptism"* for example. More so the Baptist/Black Baptist - had/was forced to - absorb a lot of Myalist theology/art forms. So the African culture/the traditions of the Peoples of west and central Africa were still very much alive. (Note, ibid, Seaga, p. 4, for polytheism perspectives in Myal and Kumina.)

which was to be read at all the sermons" for a specific time said:

> *"It, having being brought to our attention that scenes of the most indecent, degrading and superstitious character, are being enacted at August Town. We, in the virtue of the authority committed to us, by the Apostolic See, hereby ordain and command that all Catholics refrain from visiting the water at August Town, from using them or encouraging others to use them, until the restriction be withdrawn."* [156]

This was never withdrawn.

Another plantation collaborator/apologist in an article speaking upon the attitude of the Church of England, dubbed Bedward ("Black Itinerant") (as also that of **Stewart Haddo**)[157] *"superstition"*:

> *"...we are succeeding by God's blessing in training up a people many of whom have already become Christian in fact, as well as in name; intelligent, enlightened, religious, energetic, free, progressive. But what of the unreached and ignorant multitudes from which, in the main, occasional outburst of superstition like August Town and Haddo Monague water, are fed?"* [158]

One other of authority, Rev. Banbury, placed this *"water superstition"* with *"obeahism."* He said, *"..obeahism is now rife in Jamaica than ever it was ...,"* and goes on to say,

> *"....the* **water superstition** *which has sprang up since a few years ago are common (**Mother Notts** being the first*

---

[156] See **"Bishop Gordon speaks"**. (Bishop Gordon, head of the Catholic Church of Jamaica issued this circular.)

[157] **Haddo** has been mentioned already: ibid, Elkins, pp. 2-4; ibid, Mc Pherson, **The Validity of Oral History...**, pp. 114-5.

[158] See article, **"The Bedward craze and its results..."**

mover of it) [159] *[...] 1 mean as regards to the water cures! The present Mona water craze is the most remarkable we have had, in writing we had almost forgotten the St. Ann's one which occurred over 20 years ago. But that had no guiding genius or prophet. It was looked upon then more as a mineral spring than a miraculous... We believe* **the Mona water agitation** *will soon die, perhaps before this*

Figure 16: The arrest of Bro. Alexander Bedward at "The People's March," 1921

publication left the press. [Note: this was published in 1894 and after/during which time Bedwardites grew much stronger.] It is proof that our people are ready to believe anything presented to them either, by a obeah man or anyone professing to be a prophet sent from God as Mr. Bedward does." [160] (my emphases.)

---

[159] *The Author* has not yet verified who is this **"Mother Nott."**

[160] Ibid, Banbury, pp. iii-iv.

In the eyes of many, Bedwardism was "superstitious" ('obeah'). To the obeahman, "obayo" (which means "witch"), Bedward/"*The August Town water*" was indeed a "balm"/"healing stream"/ "good magic" which countered/ destroyed their "bad magic."

In an article titled, **"The full confession of the great obeahman, old George Elleth - a native of Hampton Rd. in Porus,"** (printed in the late 19th century). Elleth,

> "*.. an African whose father was an obeahman, his grandfather the greatest obeahman in his country since he began working.. 42 years* [ago], *during that time he killed* [251] *two hundred and fifty one persons, put down six hundred and fifty five* [655] *to suffer...*"

He, Elleth threatened death upon Bedward, saying

> "*1 wonder if it was not the August Town water, but if I was in Kingston as other obeahman I would kill Alexander Bedward, for from since this August Town healing stream has been found out, I lost many of my customers from Manchester, Porus, Four Paths and the rest of Alley and May Pen, Old Harbour, Chapleton, Rock River.*" [161] *.....The*

---

[161] See B. Pullen Burry, **Ethiopia in exile - Jamaica revisited**, (London), pp. 142-3. He noted Bedward "adherence" are spread all over the island. "Beside his chief chapel in August Town, there are others in various positions at Port Antonio and in Clarendon. I hear his ministration are much in request."

His "fillials"/camp-in Clarendon must have borne effects upon the obeahmen, thus leaving him [Elleth] to, state so many places in Clarendon itself (: Four Paths, Alley, May Pen, Chapleton, Rock River) as areas where he had lost customers.

Ibid, Brooke, p. 8: "While Bedward has his center in August Town, there are fillials called camps throughout the island. Each camp has its camp of workers observing the customary Divine Services and distinguishingly the fast service, tri-weekly and the vow ceremony. The... camps showed their allegiance to the present church by periodical visits to Union camp, August Town."

This "cellular structured organisation" spread afar to Central America, as in Port Limon-Costa Rico, Panama, Hondurus; and from taped interview John confirms: "36 thousand members The Church has, 125 Outstations: Panama, Colon, Bogota, Cuba. ..: All 'The Church of God' New Testament; All are Bedward's and him don't call one." (Ibid, McPherson, **The Validity of....**, p. 143.)

thing that set me mad was Sarah Smith yard. I go one day to work for her and when I had finished work, I asked her to give me some water to wash my hand and she gave me this August Town water and from since I feel the Devil in my heart... Mr. James Williams was sick for ten years and it was this Elleth that give him it and he could not get better and until he came to the August Town healing stream, but at this time Mr. James did not know that it was the obeah-man did it and still (until) a few weeks ago Mr. James was coming from the stream and meet this obeah-man and he asked him for a drink and Mr. James gave him the ram and he said to me James I want to see you. When I return I will come to your house. He said I'm sorry for what I had done you... I was going to kill a minister daughter. I put duppy on her because she met me one day in the street and did not speak to me but someone gave her some of the August Town water and from since then She is now better..."

Thus, as "Revivalists" Bedward/The Bedwardites relate to this study on obeah. Such a Black Church was not evilous, superstitiously based . Instead, this Black Church was a resurged symbol of the Myal movement cloaked in orthodox Christianity as the J.N.F.B.C./"Black Baptist's." [162]

---

[162] Such achievements were not through "spells," as some would describe it/would have us believe: (ibid, B. Pullen, p. 144:) "...so great is the spell which attract them."

Such was an ordered "Black Church" combating "witchcraft"/ "native superstition."

Continuing Revival/Black Baptist Revolt: "Warrior" Higgins – "Mass Charlie"

Early after his arrival in Jamaica from England, Rev. Captain Charlie C. Higgins, B. A. E. (British and American Evangelist) held lectures to crowds of large numbers. For example, one night while lecturing at the Victoria Gardens, downtown Kingston, in 1897, he had stated

> *"...who ever know that I had not converted [them] please do not come near me.. If you will not take heed in what I'm telling you I expect to beat it into you."*

He called himself *"King Higgins"*; the *"Black Champion."* The People called him *"Mass Charlie"*; *"Warrior" Higgins.*

At another nightly lecture this *Street-Preacher* - Black-Baptist *"Warrior Higgins,"* denounced the Roman Catholic church and Protestant ministers. Someone in the audience objected in a menacing way. The preacher collared the person and demanded, without success, that a constable arrest him. Becoming excited the crowd pressed inward. A constable whistle sounded and the Sergeant Major upon coming forward, adjourned the meeting.

Higgins irately refused, saying: *"'I defy the man to remove me.'"* He threw down his waistcoat, dragged a stick and hurled it in the air. A wrestle ensued.

The preacher was forced to submit and was taken to Sutton Street goal. In lock up he sang a favorite hymn of non-conformist missionaries: *"There is a fountain filled with blood."*

Figure 16: Street Preacher: *Lack Baptist "Warrior Higgins"*

The next night Higgins led a procession - complete with banner and band - to the Victoria Gardens, while waving a long sword in his hand, he waved the crowd back while the band played ***"Onward Christian soldier."*** On meeting the arresting Sergeant Major (from the previous night) he saluted him with his sword!

On another night, some months later, a gang of men/boys struck him with sticks, while insulting him. On his way home, they stopped him at Jubilee Market. He received a number of blows. Higgins drew a revolver and fired a shot in the air. Two plainclothes Constables tried to arrest him but his followers arrived and they pulled the Constables away. He ran to safety in a nearby house. A general fight ensued involving several hundred persons. Higgins said such was a police/gang lead - plan upon him.

In 1899 Higgins started **the Royal Millennium Baptist Missionary Society** called **the "Millennium Band"** by the people which had their grand baptism on April 9, 1899. He later began **the "Millennium Hospital,"** an upstairs flat with shop below, where he treated patients with special tonics made from herbs.

He told a newsman that the hospital had connections with **the Royal Millennium Missionary Lodge of Surrey, England**, whose members sought

> **"..to preach the gospel of religion, to be the means of receiving and aiding other people who may be sick and needing formal assistance and generally to be of some good to the poor who are unable to keep themselves."** [163] (my emphases.)

Higgins's doctrine of "baptism" saw him and Bedward hold joint baptism at times in Hope River. He said

> *"Higgins and Bedward... were taking all the black people and filling up the King's Kingdom. People by them were baptised by the people of God. I can make the Roman Catholic and the Church of England go to the river and baptise... If they don't baptise there God will send his damnation and destroy the city."*

There was a break between the two (Higgins and Bedward), as Higgins challenged *"the prophets"* right to call himself Bishop, and charged Bedward Chief Minister, **Rev C. C. Carr** of being old and incompetent to properly perform.

Higgins's oratory gave rise to public complaints in the late 1901. He, for example, reversed *"God save the King,"* to *"King save God"*; and he stated that, *"..the richer minister and judge*

---

[163] Similar to the Bedwardites, "financial obligations" were light. In Bedward's Movement a yearly ticket for membership of one shilling and three pence at the Holy Communion sometimes was called for.

There is no baptismal fee. "In some camps there is a special fee to meet the financial expenses of the poor members. The sick are cared for and momentarily distressed people continually have to be helped, by A[..] Bedward personally, Union Camp..."

were, the more foolish they became." In 1902 he called the Bishop of Jamaica, *"..a dumbed lazy idle dog,"* while he said

> *"..the Popes and the Bishops are a damned confounded liars ... They lead the people down to hell and God cried out 'who should I send to stop these things' and no one went until at last Charles Higgins."*

After one of his oratory feasts he was beaten and never revived. He died in July, 1902.

The post was filled by **Teacher Nixon**. [164]

Other **Black Baptists** as **Isaac Tate** became just as "militant" (though to a different extent less physical) by diverting from traditionalist Baptist orthodoxy. In 1896 Tate refused to administer the sacrament to smokers and drinkers. He was called upon by the Jamaica Baptist Union to resign but he himself left the union and formed **the Holiness Society** (which did not smoke, drink, eat pork, drink coffee or wear jewelry not even wedding rings. [165]

All of this Protestant sectarian movement from the established churches/theology saw **the Welch Revivalist** beginning in Jamaica in 1904-5; [166] **The Holiness Society**, frag-

---

[164] See W. F. Elkins, "Warrior Higgins A Jamaican Street Preacher," **Jamaica Journal**, Vol. 8 No. 4, pp. 28, 31; ibid, Elkins, **Street preacher...**, pp. 19-326; ibid, Mc Pherson, **The Validity...**, pp. 124-5.

[165] Ibid, Elkins, **Street Preacher...**, p. 26; ibid, Mc Pherson, **The Validity...**, pp. 125-6.

[166] Ibid, W. Wedenoja, p. 15. The "Orthodox and Revival Churches are controlled by authoritarian leader who compelled members to accept rigid dogma and rituals," while (p. 157) Pentecostal Members are forbidden to see Doctors or Healers, to wear Jewelry, go to beauty shops etc.

He also makes some comparison of these Black Church "in contrast to balm, obeah and de Laurence are regarded as a moral if not immoral," and noted that Obeah and de Laurence are illegal (as versus Revival Zion and Puku/Balms). He further concluded (on p. 158) only revivalist have little need for science, as their religion offers comparable benefits. It is Pentecostal and orthodox Christians - despite stern injunctions... who seek out practitioners of science."

menting to **Pentecostals; the Zioness** stressing seven times

---

Wedenoja's above statement were proceed before in his work by an **Anglican Church Bulletin-Balm Town**, which stated among other things: "Be aware of the revival of the Powers of Satan... We see it in the revival of spiritual-ism and the desire to be in touch with duppies. Even Christians are found to be consulting Obeah men and women, seeking for charms and spells to get their own way."

In concluding this section of Our **From "THE BLACK CHURCHES..."... BOOK ONE**, it would be instructive to readers to see Wedenoja's p. 34 fig. 41: **A Taxonomy of Religious Organisation:**

Types of spirituality Churches
Spiritual churches Normal big church
Evangelical churches Pentecostal
Revival Church of God
Jesus Only Apostolic Revival cults
Revival churches Temporal science
De Laurence Obeah
Actual copy

<table>
<tr><td colspan="9">TYPES OF SPIRITUALITY</td></tr>
<tr><td colspan="9">CHURCHES</td></tr>
<tr><td rowspan="3">NORMAL BIG CHURCH</td><td rowspan="3">EVANGELI-CAL CHURCHES</td><td colspan="4">SPIRITUAL CHURCHES</td><td rowspan="3"></td><td colspan="2" rowspan="2">TEMPORAL SCIENCE</td></tr>
<tr><td colspan="2">PENTECOSTAL</td><td colspan="2">REVIVAL</td></tr>
<tr><td>CHURCH OF GOD</td><td>JESUS ONLY APOSTOLIC</td><td>REVIVAL CULTS</td><td>REVIVAL CHURCHES</td><td>DELAURENCE</td><td>OBEAH</td></tr>
</table>

Also read Mervyn Alleyne, **"The history of African religion in Jamaica (Paper presented at the 15th Conference of Caribbean Historians, UWI, Mona, Jamaica, April 15-20, 1983),"** pp. 19-20.

He noted, that churches as Anglican, Methodist, Moravians, Presbyterian and Seven Day Adventists who reject "the practice of 'spirit possession' while Pentecostal Holiness, Shiloh Apostolic Faith, Bible Church of God 'allow the practice of spirit Possession" '(this group he calls 'self-professed Christian churches'). He next noted, "Spiritual Christian groups" as puku and revival (Zion) saying puku allows only Christian powers to possess members while Zion "allow the spirits of the departed (ancestor worship possession)." [See **Diagram** above.]

baptism before being blessed; and the (visible) beginning of **the Puku Society** in 1902 . All these Afro-Christian Black Churches are within themselves, symbols of the revivalist spirit.

It is thus not surprising that, "**the 1903 Annual Police Report** *equated Higginism along with Revivalism, obeahism and Bedwardism, as bothersome problems.*" The fear for obeah felt by the ruling class was reflected in **an Act** of **1903**, prescribing flogging as one of the penalties for practicing obeah.

❁ ❁ ❁

Part Three: Concluding Remarks

As we stated in the preface, **"Ethiopianist churches"** are "those African transferred and implanted 'Black Churches' in Jamaica; that independent 'Black Church Movement' of African and Afro-Jamaicans Creole churches that broke from white control ecclesiastically." (1) [167] It follows that this book, **From "THE BLACK CHURCHES....,"** is a symbol of an evolved "ethical alternative" by exiled Africans to white racism, white theology, Euro-Western Christianity. This represents an alternative model of development: a developed paradigm: solution.

This alternative model of development and *renewed* cultural assertion is what the Rastafari Culture was to later define as **"Black Supremacy": "Ethiopian Sovereignty"; African Ascendancy**!

Here now, at this juncture, this collective cultural assertion, seen through a 'religious' eye was dubbed: **the Black Churches**.

This **"BOOK ONE"** showed exiled Africans counter-cultural weapon against "fragmentation"; we have shown how the Black Churches/religion - has led to the preservation and subtle institutionalization of African Spirituality in *'the New World.'*

The Black Churches acted as/are serving as - a seed for African culture in the New World; a survival mechanism for assertion and liberation, and the preservation of the African personality.

In this quest let us note that "syncretism" - a dialectic of European oriented thinking - was made fertile by the enslaved and exiled Africans (so called *'slaves'* and *'ex-slaves'*).

Our Ancestors had the ideal hope of creating/ recreating - a natural society: a whole society. This was *a movement* aimed

---

[167] See Our **PREFACE**.

at bringing to fruition the genuine adaptation of African culture: Africa - into the Jamaican society.

These Black Churches took the strategic and tactical path of "interculturation" so as to in-plant themselves within the collective psyche of *the People.*

Now - these Black Churches were realistic in their "indiginizing" of black theology. For as Kwame Bresu Ando quite rightly puts it,

> "that for religion to be meaningful it should be authentic and indigenous. Such religion should not impose different and meaningless cultural ethic-ways which have nothing to do with religiousness as such."
> [168]

The European missionaries never really made any attempt to indiginize the theology of "the church," and even more so, its liturgical life. *Hence, Christianity has remained for many the "native church of the conqueror."* [169]

Black Churches were thus symbolic of a renewed religious interpretation.

Within this cultural-contact/"cultural clash" between Africans and Europeans on the Jamaican plantation, there resulted a specific missionary approach and a organic collective reaction by Africans. This process was characterized by "selective giving": "selective conservatism" on the part of Africans, who accepted and adopted mainly those elements of *the new culture*, that fit into his/her old system. There was also a selective giving on the part of the European.[170]

---

[168] Ibid, Max Assimeng, "Crisis, identity and integration in African religion" in Hans Mol, **Identity and religion**, p. 111.

[169] See Knolly Clarke, "Liturgy and culture in the Caribbean," in **Troubling of the waters - a collection of papers presented at two conferences on creative theological reflection held in Jamaica on the 3rd-4th May, 1973, p. 142and in Trinidad on the 28th-30th May, 1973**, p. 142.

[170] See Bengt G. M. Sundkler, **Bantu Prophets in South Africa**, (Oxford University Press), first published 1948, p. 296.

Above all, Black Churches while being "un-bashfully religious" were conduits for/a womb for revolt - revolution - revolutionary politics!

It is a fact that we inherited certain religious culture from Africa that entailed **a "religious political culture."** In Jamaica, Obeah galvanized slave revolts and became "the coat of religion for black culture" as symbolized by **Tacky's 1760 intercommunal revolt.**

In the Akan culture, for example, the word, *"obe,"* means *"to heal,"* and the healer is at the same time *"a priest."* In Africa - generally speaking - *high ESP - extra sensory perception people* are brought into *"the center of the culture"* - into *"The Priesthood."* Thus, in the Akan culture, the *"Acumfondche"* is a *Healer, Priest* and *Politician* who held together the Ashanti confederacy; and, he was *a Warrior who goes into battle.*

Thus, **Tacky**, was *a 'slave driver'* (*'leader of men'*) for the plantation, but *under-the-surface* he is an **"Obeahman"** to his colleagues!

Therefore, his *atomic multi-personality* manifested his political and military aptitudes, and revealed the African culture - unmasked/*above-ground* - activity in the daylight. This is a symbolic emergence of African culture re-emerging to the surface; **a first in Caribbean history!**

The **Sam Sharpe 'Christmas Rebellion': "revolt/"the Black Baptist/Myalist War"** was another example of a "radical political" uprising - the preservation of the culture from *the Church "womb."* Thus, through what seemed like 'secular revolts', to collective revolts, revolt - revolution and radical politics trod on through the Black Churches. There was for example, the **Kenecuffes - Nanny - Cudjoe: The Maroons** and **"The Black Baptist-Myalist War" of 1832/3**; to intercommunal revolts as Tacky's, to the 1890s-1920s **"Peoples' Church" of Bedward** - a response to Crown Colony Government of 1865 and a symbol of "communalist nationalism."

The question of the white plantation/Euro-Western "ethnocentrism," qualifications/ dis-qualifications of African religious forms, "Black Churches," as expressions/emanations of 'obeah' throughout the histography, needs to be looked into.

"Obeah," was legally arrested by the plantocracy in 1760: by the beginning of the 19th century obeah and myal were deemed to be one and the same - by these "cultural censors"; and, by 1904, revival movements, Bedwardites, Higginism and obeah were all equated to be one and the same illegal groups.

Even with the high visibility of the religious forms of the Myalist period, the "positive magic" of Myal was decried by Europeans and ignorant prying creoles. In fact, the word, *'magic'*, to the white man, meant the Peoples' Culture was not taken seriously. All of which was furthered and compounded by no English word being able to describe best the African religious experiences!

Thus M. G. Lewis noted rightly that it was difficult for the plantation

> "to know if the slave had any religious beliefs or practices since the only external signs of a 'priest' was the obeahman. However, this was so as it was in Africa and now in the Caribbean, religion was not externalised or institutionalised. The obeahman was thus a doctor, philosopher and priest. Healing was in a sense an act of faith... and the fetish (suman) had come to mediate... likewise man and God... was regarded as an attribute token of the God. Each man... in a way not understood by Europeans was a priest and through possession induced by communal dancing to drum, could communicate with the God and assume the God." [171]

Notwithstanding this warped perception of whites, it is a universal fact that all religions have an element of *the surreal,* i. e., they aim at expressing the subconscious mind, and thus many words used by the plantocracy (and present Euro-

---

[171] See Gordon K. Lewis, **The Growth of the Modern West Indies**, (Modern Readers Publication, New York and London), 1968, p. 219.

Western theologians) to describe the African phenomena are not right. [172]

Black Churches, beginning with Obeah, have pointed to many personality types, of the plantation, that still abound with us today. There remains:

the **"Quashie"** type, *'the good nigger'*;

the **"Anancy/Ananci"** type, that *'clever nigger'* who manipulated his environment and never lost control of situations;

and above all, **the "Rebel"** types:

(i) **would be rebels** - *Calliband,*

(ii) **Rebel** as Tacky,

(iii) **Maroon rebel** - physical as Nanny (in history books) and psychological as portrayed by Estaband Montejo, **"Diary of a run away slave,"** among others.[173]

From "THE BLACK CHURCHES"..., we see clearly "a unity of morality" based on/in "righteousness," actively dealing with the question of selfhood and nationhood through traditional theories of African culture and religion.

In **"BOOK TWO"** this unity of the Black Churches (cultural integration) leads to the uprising of the **Rastafari Faith/ Culture** [174] from the cultural crossroads/juncture of **the Bedwardites** and **Garvey's U.N.I.A.'s - A.O.C./ African Orthodox**

---

[172] I continue to Honor [now **Prof.] Dr E. K. Brathwaite's, "H303 - History, society and ideas in the British Caribbean, lectures of 1981-2,"** especially as they related to **Religion(s): The Black Churches**.

[173] Op. cit. Other **"personality types"** in the Caribbean - seen through the histographic life of the plantation - ex-plantation and Black Churches are **(i) submerged types** - not allowed to/do not fulfil their potential(s) - doesn't achieve level of visibility; **(ii) Ariel, free coloreds**, these self-haters deluded are seen in Derrick Walcott's, **A far cry from Africa**, and **Dream on Monkey Mountain**; **Miranda**, as seen in Prospero's daughter (C. I. A. element).

Again Prof. Brathwaite's literary historic analysis and synthesis has assisted greatly in identifying the different personality types, and is a prism to be further exploited by readers.

[174] Ibid, E. S. P. Mc Pherson, **From "The Black Churches to The Nyahbinghi Order - the Youth Black Faith,"** pp. 53-95; pp. 112-217.

Church, pooling out into the emergence of the earliest histographic growth of **Rastafari**.

These Black Churches are also haunted with the ever persistent specter of *'obeah'*, carried out by the mis-qualifications of "ethnocentrists." The survival, existence and growth of these Black Churches implied, and called for, the destruction of an oppressing status quo (throughout history). And this is why *the-powers-that-be* continually seek to marginalize their specific rites, rituals, organizational formations, and collective activities towards self determination (Governance).

Bibliography to Concluding Remarks

Anon, **Hamel the obeahman 2 vols.**, (London) 1807.

Assimeng, Max, "Crisis, identity and integration in African religion" in ibid, Hans Mol (ed.) **Identity and religion**.

Brathwaite, E. K. **"Typology; Wars of respect; Caliban, Ariel and Unprospero."**

Clarke, Knolly, "Liturgy and culture in the Caribbean," in, (ldris Hamid - Edited), **Troubling of the waters - a collection of papers presented at two conferences on creative theological reflection held in Jamaica on the 3rd –4th and in Trinidad on the 28th -30th May, 1973** pp. 141-164.

Lectures of (**Prof.**) **Dr. E. K. Brathwaite, H303/History, society and ideas in the British Caribbean**, (Mona, UWI, Kingston, Jamaica), 1981-2.

Lectures of **Dr Horace Russell, Development of civilization on Religion**, (Mona, UWI, Kingston, Jamaica), 1980-1.

Lewis, Gordon K., **The Growth of the modern West Indies** (Modern Readers Publication, New York and London), 1968.

Lecturer - guest: **Dr Sawyers (world known religionist from Africa on African religions and magic/superstition)**, (at the Development of Civilization course Lectures of Dr Russell at Mona, UWI, Kingston, Jamaica), 1981-2.

Mc Pherson, E. S. P., **From "The Black Churches" to -The Nyahbinghi Order - The Youth Black Faith,"** (H305 Course, M. Phil. Qualification project presentation, History Department, Mona, UWI, Kingston, Jamaica), May 1983.

Montejo, Esteban, **The autobiography of a runaway slave**.

Rohler, Gordon, "Man's spiritual search in the Caribbean through literature," in ibid, ldris Hamid (ed.), **Troubling of the waters...**, pp. 187-205.

Sundkler, Bengt G. M., **Bantu prophets in South Africa**, (Oxford University Press), first published 1948.

Walcott, Derrick, **What the twilight says**; Walcott, Derrick, **Dream on Monkey Mountain, A far cry from Africa**.

Note: On the previous page: Anon, Hamel, **The obeahman**, is the first in Caribbean literature and history that an "Obeahman"/ "African" is the central character; this is a symbol of a literate breakthrough for the African culture, ibid, Mc Pherson, **The Validity of oral history...**, p. 110.

Bibliography to Original Text

Published Books, Journals, Magazines

Augier, Roy, M. G. Smith and Rex Nettleford, **The Rastafari movement in Kingston, Jamaica,** (Kingston, UWI,ISER),1960.

Assimeng, Max, "Crisis, identity and integration in African religion," in, Hans Mol (Edited) **Identity and religion international cross-cultural approaches**, (Sage Publications Inc., 275 South Beverly Drive, Beverly Hills, California 90212/ Sage studies in international sociology), 1978.

Banbury, **Rev. R. Thomas, Jamaica superstition or the obeah book, a complete treatise of the absurdities believed in by the people of the island Jamaica**, (Martiner L. De Souza, printer, 7 Charles St., Jamaica),1894.

Barrett, Leonard, **The sun and the drum - African roots in Jamaican folk tradition,** (Sangster's Book Stores Ltd., Kingston, Jamaica, Heinemann), 1976.

Barrett, Leonard, **Soul Force: African heritage in Afro-American religion**, (New York), 1974; Barrett, Leonard, "Portrait of a Jamaican healer: African medical lore in the Caribbean," **Caribbean Quarterly**, Vol. 19 No. 3 (September 1973).

Beckwith, Martha, **Black roadways: A study of Jamaican folk life**, (Chapel Hill University of North Carolina Press), 1929.

Burry, B. Pullen, **Ethiopia in exile - Jamaica revisited**, (London), 1905 .

Burkett, K. Randall, **Garveyism as a religious movement**, (The Scarecrow Press and the Jersey and London), 1978.

Brathwaite, E. K., **"The Great rebellion in the Great River Valley of St James, 1831/32,"** (Mona, UWI), 1982.

Brathwaite, E. K., **The development of creole society in Jamaica 1770-1820**, (Clarendon Press, Oxford), 1971, reprinted in paper-back form, 1978.

Brathwaite, E. K., **Contradictory omens, cultural diversity and integration in the Caribbean**, (Savacou Publications, Mona) 1974, reprinted 1977.

Brathwaite, E. K., **"An evening with the status quo,"** (A Savacou working paper, Mona, UWI), 1982.

Brathwaite, Edward Kamu, "Kumina - The spirit of African survival," **Jamaica Journal**, No. 42 pp. 44-63.

Brathwaite, E. K., "Caliban, Ariel and Unprospero in the conflict of creolization - a study of the slave revolt in Jamaica in 1831-32," **Annals of the New York Academy of Sciences**, 292 (1977) pp. ...

Brathwaite, E. K., "The African presence in Caribbean literature," in Sidney Mintz (edited), **Slavery, colonialism and racism**, (New York: W. W. Norton and Co.), 1974, pp. 73-109.

Brooks, A. A., **A history of Bedwardism or the Jamaica Native Baptist Free Church**, (Kingston, The Gleaner Co. i1 second printing 1917.

Campbell, Sadie, "Bush teas, a cure all: Corollary to folklore and food habits," **Jamaica Journal** 8 (1974) pp. 60-65.

Campbell, Sadie, "Folklore and food habits," **Jamaica Journal** 8 (1974), pp. 56-59.

Cary, Beverley, "The Windward Maroons after the peace treaty," **Jamaica Journal**, Dec. 1970 Vol. 4 No. 4, p. 19.

Cassidy, Frederic, **Jamaica Talk: Three hundred years of the English language in Jamaica**, (London, Macmillan). 1961.

Cassidy, Frederic and R. B. Le Page, **The dictionary of Jamaican English**, (London, Cambridge University Press), 1967 .

Chaanaiwa, David (Edited and introduced), **Profiles of self determination - African responses to European colonialism in southern Africa 1652-present**, (California State University, Northridge), 1976.

Curtain, Philip, **Two Jamaicas: The role of ideas in a tropical colony**, 1959 (reprinted, New York, Atheneum), 1970.

Dallas, R. C., **History of the Maroons, 2 vols.**, (London, T. N. Longman and 0. Rees), 1803.

Danquau, J. B. (illustrated by Kofi Antubam of Achimota),**The Akan doctrine of God, A fragment of Gold Coast ethic and religion**, (Frank Cass and Co. Ltd.), 1968.

Delliser, G., **Twentieth century Jamaica**, (Kingston, Jamaica), 1930.

Durkheim, Emile (translated from the French by Joseph Ward Swain, M.A.), **The elementary forms of the religious life, A study in religious sociology**, (London, Gercer Arew and Unwin; New York, The Macmillian Company),1965.

Elkins, W. F., **"Street preacher, faith healer and herb doctor in Jamaica, 1890-1925"** (Revisionist Press, New York), 1977.

Elkins, W. F., "'Warrior' Higgins, A Jamaican street preacher," **Jamaica Journal**, Vol. 8 No. 4.

Forsythe, Dennis, **"West Indian culture through the prism of Rastafarism,"** (Dept of Sociology, UWI, Mona), 1979.

Gamache, Henri, **Mystery of the long lost 8th, 9th and 10th book of Moses together with the legend that was of Moses and 44 secret keys to universal power**, (Sheldon Publications, Highland Falls, New York), 1967 4th printing.

Gardner, W. J., **History of Jamaica**, (London), 1873.

Haughton, Robert, "African conversion," **Africa**, Vol. 41, 1971, pp. 96-7.

Harris, T., "'Boots', gospel myalism," **Roots News**, Vol. 2, October-November (B & J Production Ltd.), pp. 1, 50.

Henriques, Fernando, **Jamaica**.

Higgman, Barry, **Slave population and economy in Jamaica 1807-1834**, (London, Cambridge University Press), 1976.

Hill, Dr Robert A., "Dread history: Leonard P. Howell and Millenarian visions in early Rastafari religions in Jamaica," **Yard Roots** Black History Monday, Vol. 1 No. 4,, 1982, pp. 12-16.

Hoetink, K., "The concept of pluralism as envisaged by M. G. Smith," **Caribbean Studies**, April 1967).

Critiques of plural society" in **Caribbean Studies** 7:1(1%7): Caribbean race relations.

Hogg, Donald, "The Convince cult in Jamaica," in S. Mintz (compiled), **Papers in Caribbean anthropology**, (New Haven), 1960.

Herskovits, M. J., **The myth of the negro past**, (New York), 1966.

Herskovits, M. J., **The New World negro**, (Bloomington, Indiana, Indiana University Press), 1966.

ldowu, E., Bolaji, **Olodumane god in Yoruba belief**, (Longman), 1962.

Jamaica Journal, Vol. 16 Nos. Feb. 1983, p. 34.

Jamaica Law 5 of 1898, The Obeah Law 1898, p. 65.

Journal of the Jamaican House of Assembly, Vols. iii & iv. .

Lane, Carl, "Concerning Jamaica 1760 slave rebellions," **Jamaica Journal**, Dec 1973, Vol. 7 No. 4 pp. 24.

Laurence, De, **The sixth and seventh books of Moses**, (printed in the USA).**The great book of magical art, Hindu magic and east Indian occultism**, (1898).

Laurence, De, **The book of secret Hindu ceremonial and Talismanic magic**;

Laurence, De, **The Master Key**.

Lewis, Gordon K., **The growth of the modern West Indies**, (Modern Reader Paperbacks, New York and London), 1968.

Lewin, Olive, "Underlying values in traditional conimunications," **Communications and information for development purposes in the Caribbean area**, (International Broadcast Institute Ltd.) 1975, pp. 16-19.

Linyard, Fred, **The Moravians in Jamaica from the beginning to emancipation 1754-1838**.

Long, Edward, **History of Jamaica, 3 vols**., (London),1787.

Maragh, G. G., **The Promise Key**, (The Harding Commercial Pri ntry, 28 George Lane, Kingston) in Dr. Nnamdi Azikiwe (edited), The African Morning Post, Head Office, Accra, Gold Coast.

Martin, Tony, **Race first - The ideological and organizational struggles of Marcus Garvey and the United Negro Improvement Association**, (Greenwood Press),1976.

Mathurin, Lucille (illustrated by Dennis Ranston), **The rebel woman in British West Indies during slavery**, (Africa-Caribbean Publications, 1975.

Mbiti, John S., **African religions and philosophy,** (Anchor Books Doubleday and Company Inc., Garden City, New York, 1970.

Mc Pherson, E.S.P., **Brother Bedward - A reasons presented by E. S. P. Mc Pherson B.A. (Hon.) (UWI) at the Chapleton and District Historical Society public meeting, Thursday 24th of May, 1984, 7.00 p.m. at Salem United Church, Chapleton, Jamaica**, (Black International Iyahbinghi Press, Frankfield P.O., Clarendon, Jamaica), March 1985.

Mc Pherson, E.S.P., **Brother Bedward**, (Black International Iyahbinghi Press, Frankfield P.O. Boy 15, Clarendon, Jamaica), 1984 March.

Mc Pherson, E.S.P., **The Most Honorable "Marcus" upon South Africa/Azania**,(Black International lyahbinghi Press, Frankfield P.O., Clarendon, Jamaica), February 1984; July 1984.

Mc Pherson, E. S. P. and L. T. Semaj, "Rasta chronology," **Caribbean Quarterly**, Vol. 26 No. 4 December 1980, foreword pages, pp. 97-8 (released 1982), reprinted Monograph, 1985, pp. 116-9.

Mc Pherson, Ras Everton, *"Rastafari: An Open Challenge To 'The Church',"* **METRO EXCHANGE the arts & culture news magazine [USA]** (Edited by Lori Thompson-Reid; Copy Chief: Charles P. Dougherty), Vol. 8 NO. 4 APRIL 1995, pp. 1,3-4, 6, 15.

Mol, Hans (edited), **Identity and religion international cross- cultural approaches**.

Montejo, Esteban, **Autobiography of a runaway slave**, (Harmondsworth - Penguin Books, 1970.

Moore, J. G. and G. E. Simpson, **A comparative study of acculturation in Morant Bay and west Kingston, in Zaire**, (1957, 1958).

Moorish, Ivor, **Obeah, Christ and Rastaman - Jamaica and its religions**, (James Clarke and Co.), 1982.

Napier, Robert, "The first arrest of Bedward," **Jamaica Historical Society Bulletin**, 111 March 1957.

Patterson, Orlando, **The sociology of slavery: An analysis of the origins, development and structure of negro slave society in Jamaica**, (Rutherford, N. J. - Fairleigh Dickinson University Press), 1969.

Pettazzon, Raffacle (authorized translation by H. J. Rose), **The all-knowing god researches into early religions and culture**.

Phillipo, James M., **Jamaica: Its past and present state**, (1843; reprinted, London, Faber and Faber), 1969 .

Price, Richard (Edited), **Maroon Societies: Rebel slave communities in the America**, (Garden City, Doubleday, Anchor Press),1973.

Redfield, **Robert, Peasant society and culture**, (University of Chicago Press), 1956.

Reynolds, C. Roy, "Tacky and the great slave rebellion in the 1760," **Jamaica Journal**, June 1972 Vol. 6 No. 2 pp. 5-8.

Robertson, Diane, **Jamaican herbs nutritional and medicinal values**, (Jamaica Herbs Limited), March 1982.

Russell, Horace O., "The emergence of the Christian black concept: The making of a stereotype," **Caribbean Journal of Religion Studies**, Vol. 2 No. 1 April 1979, pp. 1-17.

Schuler, Monica, **Alas, alas, Kongo - A social history of indentured African immigration into Jamaica, 1841-1865**, (The John Hopkins University Press, Baltimore and London), 1980.

Seaga, Edward, "Revivalist cults in Jamaica - Notes towards a sociology of religion" (reprinted from **Jamaica Journal** Vol. 3 No. 2 June 1969) pp. 3-13.

Simpson, George Eaton, "Cultural change and reintegration found in cults in western Kingston, Jamaica," **Science Museum Library**, Vol. 99, No 2, April 1955, pp. 89-92.

Simpson, George Eaton, "Political cultism in western Kingston, Jamaica," **Social and Economic Studies**, (ISER, UWI), Vol. 14 No 2 Dec, 1955.

Simpson, George Eaton, **Religious cults of the Caribbean: Trinidad, Jamaica and Haiti**, (Institute of Caribbean Studies, University of Puerto Rico, Piedras, Puerto Rico 00931), second edition 1960, pp. 208-23, pp. 224-30.

Simpson, George Eaton, **The Shango cult in Trinidad** (Puerto Rico) 1965.

Simpson, George Eaton, **The African heritage 'n the Caribbean**.

Smith, M. G., The plural society in the British West Indies, (University of California Press, Berkeley and Los Angeles), 1965.

"Syllabus for examination in Caribbean history, objectives of the syllabus."

Stewart, James, "The African heritage in the Caribbean," in Vera Rubin (edited),**Caribbean Studies: A symposium** Seattle (University of Washington Press) pp. 34-45.

Tsomondo, Madziwanyika S., **"Against alienism: The response of the Zionist and apostolic independent Christian church movements to European colonialism in Zimbabwe,"** in, ibid, David Chanaiwa (Edited and introduced).

Wach, Joachim, **Sociology of religion**, (London), 1974.

Waddell, Joseph, **Voodoos and obeahs: phases of West Indian witchcraft**, (New York, Dial Press),1932.

Wallace, A. F. C., "Revitalization movements," **American Anthropologist**,1958, pp. 264-281.

William, Joseph, Psychic phenomena of Jamaica, (New York), 1934.

Wynter, Sylvia, "John Konnu in Jamaica," **Jamaica Journal**, June 1970.

Unpublished sources:

Theses Personal Papers/ Project; Presentations/Conference papers; pamphlets:

Albuquerque, Klaus De, **Millenarian movements and the politics of liberation: The rastafarians of Jamaica**, (Virginia Polythenic Institute and State University, Ph.D. 1977), Sociology, general

Alleyne, Mervyn, **"The history of African religion in Jamaica - paper presented at the Fifteenth Conference of Caribbean Historians, UWI, Mona, Jamaica, April 15-20."**

Chevannes, A. Barry, **Social Origins of Rastafari**,. (ISER, Mona, UWI) 1978.

Chevannes, Alston, **Jamaica lower class religion: Structures against oppression**, (Master's degree thesis, University of the West Indies), 1971.

Ebanks, R. C., **"The Maroons 1655-1740,"** (A personal unpublished Paper/Report),1973-4.

Eyre, Alan, Jack Mansong, "Bloodshed or brotherhood," **Jamaica Journal**, December 1973 Vol. 7 No. 4a.

Lectures of **Dr. E. K. Brathwaite**, H303/ History, societies and ideas in the British Caribbean at Mona, UWI, Kgn. Ja., 1981-2.

Lectures of **Dr. Rev. Horace Russell**, Develop-ment of civilisation, on Religion, 1980-1 at Mona, UWI, Kgn, Ja., 1981-2.

Lecture Guest **Dr. Sawyers** (World renowned religionist from Africa), **"African traditional religions and magic/superstition"**, at the Development of Civilization .

Lecture, of **Dr Horace Russell** at Mona, UWI, Kgn., Ja., 1981-2.

Lectures of **Dr. Don Robatham**, in *Anthropology of the Caribbean peoples*, at Mona, UWI, Kgn. Ja., 1986-7.

Lectures of **Dr. Barry Chevannes**, in *Caribbean Social Structure*, at Mona, UWI, Kgn, Ja., 1986-7 (on Religion).

Lectures of **Dr. Dennis Forsythe** in *Introduction to Sociology*, at Mona, UWI, Kgn, Ja., 1979-80.

Long, Joseph K., **Folk Medicine (P....D.**, Dept of Anthropology, University of California) 1973.

Mc Pherson, E. S. P., **The Validity of Oral History as a Means of Historical Investigation: A Case Study of Rastafari**, (Caribbean studies, Mona, UWI, History Department) 1982.

Mc Pherson, Everton St. P., **From "The Black Churches" to "The Nyahbinghi Order: The Youth Black Faith,"** (A H350 Course - M. Phil. Qualifying research paper, History Department, Mona, UWI), May 1983.

Mc Pherson, Everton, **An Ethnohistory Of The Rastafari Culture: The Youth Black Faith: Nyahbinghi order of His Majesty**, (A anthropology course work study - M.Sc. qualifying, Mona, UWI, Ugh. Ja.) 1985-6/86-7.

Mc Pherson, Everton, **Answer to Q.: Account for the spread of the Rastafari religion throughout the world** (A Caribbean social structure - coursework 1985-6, Mona, UWI, Kgn. Ja.)

Mc Pherson, Everton, **Answer to Q.: Compare and contrast the analysis of Carl Stone and M. G. Smith of the race question in Jamaica** (A anthropology course work essay, 1985-6, Mona, UWI, Kgn. Ja.)

Mc Pherson, E. S. P. B.A. (Hon.), **The Rt. Hon. "Marcus" Mosiah Garvey - The Black Moses and St. John The Divine, A Black Internationalist and "Philosophic Statesman's" Challenge to the State and Church, Educators and Our People - A Voice crying in the wilderness**, section called **A Challenge**, pp. 5-7, (A centenary celebration paper/unpublished letter to the editor of the Gleaner, Feb. 1987) (Frankfield P.O., Clarendon, Jamaica).

Moore, J. G., **Religion of Jamaica negroes**, (Ph.D. thesis, Northwestern University) 1953.

Nelson, Charles C. H., **"Witchcraft (ex- plantation) divination(verification),"** (A selected African project, A.C.I.J.) 30.1.81.

Roberts, Jennifer, **"The development of the Bedwardites movement,"** (Caribbean studies), 1975/76.

Shibata, Yoshika, **Rastafari music in Jamaica: Its historical and cultural significance, a study of socio-religious music in Culturalogy of area studies**, (University of Tsukuba, Japan a un-published thesis), January 1981.

Wedenjoa, W, **Religion and adaptation in rural Jamaica**, (unpublished thesis, University of California, San Diego), 1978.

Newspapers

Adams, Trevor **"Obeah makes a come back",** (Bridgetown, Barbados - Reuters), [...].

"...but the church is skeptical," (Reuters, Georgetown), Nov. 9.

Brooks, H. A. (Mrs.), 6 Bramwell Dr., Kingston 8, Oct 19, 1982,

"Revivalism," **The Daily Gleaner** (Letter to the Editor) Oct 29, 1982

Clarke, Mitize (Student, UWI), "Counteract his onslaught of Satan!," **Daily News** (Letter to the Editor Feedback), Nov 25, 1982.

Gordon, Rev Ernie, 5 Cowper Dr., Kingston 20, Hall, Billy, "Revivalism yet again!," **The Sunday, Daily Gleaner** (Church Commentary), [...], p. 16.

Billy Hall, "Roots of cults," **The Sunday Gleaner** (Church Commentary), November 7, 1982, pp. 8, 19.

"Forbes Burnham defends obeah decision," (Georgetown, Guyana), No. 7, [...].

Hearne, John, "Revival and the church," **The Daily Gleaner**, Oct 28, 1982, p. 6.

Hughes, Alister, **"Legalising obeah,"** (St. George's, Grenada), [..].

Jacobs, H. P., **"First in two part series - Obeah, culture and colonialism,"** [...].

Kitchin, Arthur, "Our national heritage," **The Daily Gleaner**, Oct 11, 1982, pp. 8-17.

Kitchen, Arthur, "Rituals and spirits," **The Daily Gleaner**, Oct. 25, 1982, p. 8.

Mentus, Ulric, "Catholic versus pro-obeahist," **Caribbean Commentary**, p. 22.

"Obeah is ancient African religious rite, Burnham," **The Daily Gleaner**, [...].

"Paper raps Guyana's bid to legalise obeah," **Sunday Express** (Port of Spain, Trinidad), Nov. 4, [...].

"Philip St John Hill, Priest explains Zion revivalism ('moving into the spirit is our most precious facility' in Religion," **Daily News**, Sun, April 17, 1983, p. 6.

Slave Pickney, "The matter of obeah," **Daily News** (Letter to the editor Feedback), [...].

"Revival and Church, **Sunday Gleaner** (letter to editor), Oct. 29, 1982, p. 18.

"Revivalism, kumina, a Christianity," **Daily News** (Letter to the Editor) (Feedback), Oct. 26, 1982.

McLeavy, Rev. B. L. Moravians Church, Betharbara Newport, Manchester, Oct. 29, 1982

Morris, Margaret, "Watt Town Revival Schoolroom," **The Sunday Gleaner Magazine**, Nov. 21, 1982, pp.1-3.

Tanna, Laura, "Kumina: The Kongo connection," **The Sunday Gleaner Magazine**, Dec. 5, 1982, p.1.

"The full confession of the great obeahman, old George Elleth - a native of Hampton Rd. in Porus," [printed in the late 19th century, Jamaica, B.W.I.]

Wint, Carl, "Can obeah ever be made respectable," **Daily News** (Nation's business) (Kingston Jamaica), [...].

Oral sources:

Informants; taped Panel Discussion, taped Interviews

Bedwardites, The, August Town, Kingston, Jamaica., 1981-2.

Boanerges, Ras, Angola - August Town, Kingston, Jamaica, 1980-6, taped and oral.

Emanuel, Bro. Prince Charles Edward [the late], Oral notes and taped reasoning, 1982-3, Bull Bay St. Thomas, Jamaica.

Henry, Bro. Roman, Taped reasoning, 1982, August Town, Kingston, Jamaica.

"Obeah, a panel discussion with Dr Nkenderig, Mr. Kofi Kayiga, Dr Liburra Ononunju, Dr E. K. Brathwaite" (UWI, ASAWI meeting) January, 1974.

Brown, Bro. Everald, Murray Mountain, St Anns, Jamaica, 1982.

Hibbert, Bro. Joseph Nathaniel [the late], St Thomas, Jamaica,1982-3.

Howellites, The, Hill 60, Salt Spring, Vere, Clarendon, Jamaica, 1982-3.

" ...Princes shall come out of Egypt; Ethiopia shall soon stretch out her hands unto God..." (Psalms 68 verse 31.)

Appendix

The Rt. Hon. "Marcus" Mosiah Garvey - The Black Moses and St. John The Divine; A Black Nationalist, and "Philosophic Statesman's" Challenge to the State and Church, Educators and Our People: A Voice Crying Out in the Wilderness

Figure 17: The Rt. Hon. Marcus Mosiah Garvey "A Voice Crying in the Wilderness"

....A challenge

.....This then is The Challenge to the church!

1) To see to it that Marcus Garvey's teachings and philosophies are fully incorporated into the curriculum of tertiary institutions and all other levels of the educational system. Meaning, in the secondary and primary schools - at the **C.X.C. Examination "A"** and **"0"** levels; at **the J. S. C. Examination level**; at **the Common Entrance** level and in infant schools - aide by teaching tools.

2) To accept and practice - faithfully - the black perspective of Marcus Garvey's *black theology*; and, do the same with other liberation theology that our historical circumstances have borne. This spiritual fruition has given rise to a diverse pantheon of Black Churches in Jamaica, a country reputed to have the most churches per square mile in the world.

The acceptance and faithful practice of Marcus's black liberation theology will stop the ensuing rivalry and non-issue of Established churches vs (neo) Evangelicals vs (neo) Pentecostals etc.. This official acknowledgement would instead give recognition and credence to the cultural and theistic diversities of these black churches, so that, *"the gospel of liberation, freedom and equality"* trod on in strength.

The theology to respond to Marcus Garvey's black theology, need not, to be now hurriedly shaped, as, this *"gospel of liberation"* has long been created, from the days of [**K/Cush** to **KMT/Kemet**] *"Moses to Christ."*

How does the contemporary Jamaican churches now react to Marcus Garvey being canonized by *the "Afro-Athlican Constructive Gaathly" Church/The Hamatic Church* (as it was called in Jamaica)? [175]

---

[175] See Dr. Tony Martin, "Some reflections on evangelical Pan Africanism or black missionaries, white missionaries and the struggle for African souls," **Ufahmu** (Winter 1971): 84; Dr. Tony Martin, Race **first, the ideological and organizational struggles of Marcus Garvey and the Universal Negro Improvement Association**, p. 78; Dr. Robert Hill, "Leonard P. Howell and Millenarian vision in

How would they react to the then contemporary UNIA divisions defying Marcus Garvey? Do these theologians know that a praxis of the UNIA is that *"...the Association is for the purpose of embracing every [Ethiopian/African] negro regardless of whatever creed or religion."* [176]

So while there is schismatic squabbling among the differing fundamental denominations of Orthodox Christianity in Jamaica and the continuing persistent perversity to prevent Marcus Garvey's teaching and philosophies (especially his black theology), the UNIA has been way ahead theistically in the propounding of *the true "gospel of liberation"*; they have been getting on with the matter at hand: *Praising the Lord.*

Let the voice of the **"Black Moses"** echo in the church: *"There is nothing wrong with Christianity. It is the purest philosophy of all time. There is nothing wrong with Christ. The evil is with the damned rascals who have been using Christianity to feather their own nest."*; [177] *"...I am...a Christian and a firm believer in the Godhead..."* [178]

Let the voice of the **"Black Moses - St John The Divine"** and the UNIA echo in these *"edifices called churches"* through the resolutions of the Seventh International Convention of the Negro People of the World held under the auspices of the UNIA, Aug 1-31, 1934 at Kingston, Jamaica, BWI upon religion

> "...Be it resolved that this convention go on record as endorsing and recognising the doctrine of Jesus Christ known as Christianity and that this convention encourages negroes all over the world to request of their respective denominations the highest form of spiritual worship so that the Christian religion to which we dedicate our religious conceptions may be

---

early Rastafari," **Jamaica Journal Quarterly of the Institute of Jamaica**, Vol. 16 No. I February 1983 pp. 226-7.

[176] See **The Black Man**, Vol. IV, Feb 1939 No. 1 p. 9.

[177] See **The Black Man**, Vol. 1, Late March, 1936, No. 12 p. 12.

[178] See **The Black Man**, Vol. ii, Aug., 1937, No. 7, p. 2O.

applied to our everyday life and uplift in keeping with the divine will."

"....1) The following resolution was submitted by delegate Haynes of Philadelphia: Whereas religion is the most dynamic force in the evolution and advancement of individuals, races and nations and..

Whereas this force because of its emotional appeal and spiritual idealism, has been commercialised and ruthlessly exploited in perpetuating ignorance, superstition and stupidity among the masses of mankind and

Whereas religion can either be an opiate or an inspiration depending upon the usage's to which it is applied and

Whereas the [Ethiopian/African] has suffered greatly from religious fanaticism and commercialisation....

Be it resolved that members of the race be implored to regard with reverence and seriousness the fundamental tenets of all recognised religions that believe in the one Supreme God in addition to the Christian religion; that whatever their religious conviction are they translate them into articulate, practical and sober service to their fellowmen.

And be it resolved that we implore members of the race to acquire an intelligent conception of the God they worship as well as an intelligent, interpretation of the Bible and other recognised religious text books, that negroes make of their religion a fountain of inspiration rather than a valley of tears, lamentations and fear; that members of the race conceive their deity as a spirit not foreign to their own traditional religious practice, to think of this deity in physical form, his image and likeness be dramatized in the physical beauty and religious literature and propaganda not contained in the Bible be philosophies to the spiritual life of the race..."[179]

So again, another challenge to the Jamaican churches:

3) is for an agreed upon implementation of an interdenominational approach among the whole ecumenical community of Christian churches, Traditional (Black) Churches and World religions - represented here in Jamaica. Such would demand of all, the exercise of "tolerance" towards each other. It would further demand knowledgeable analyses and critiques to be presented about formerly "silenced" aspects of *the gospel* - **The Bible** and other relevant (unincorporated) religious/philosophic literate sources. (And here it must be noted that these sources tend to be unincorporated by respective Christian denominations/Euro-Western theology; and, many of these unincorporated sources are on the government banned book list; or, are only accessible to and affordable by an "educated elite" of Jamaicans.)

4) The Jamaican society is now challenged to now see fit, *The Spirit*, akin to Our self image, as Ethiopians/African, which relates to the demographic reality of a 98 per cent African majority. In this new theocentric focus to be actualized/practised by the Jamaican society, there should be a respectful submission to *the universality of "The Supreme God"* - which is thus "transcultural" and multiracial in existence.

So the UNIA having black Jews, "Black Baptists," Muslims, traditional African religionists, Masons [180] and the whole array of orthodox Christian denominations had/have achieved what the contemporary Jamaican churches have not! The UNIA gave (re-) birth to *A Church Of One Foundation; A Church* that was/ is non-exclusionist, and non-schismatic in behavior. This was *A Universal Church* that was/is cosmocentric/theocentric in by qualifications.

---

[179] See the **Black Man**, Vol. 1, Nov. 1934 pp. 24-5.

[180] See Theodore G. Vincent, **Black Power and the Garvey Movement**, pp. 157-8.

This was a symbol of *A Universal Church*!. Thus befittingly, in truth, and through actions, the UNIA's African anthem thundered:

> *"...Jahova, the Great One has heard us,*
> *He has noted our sighs and our tears/*
> *With His Spirit of Love has stirred us/*
> *to be one through the coming years..."* [181]

So the refusal of the UNIA to exclusively adopt any single religous denomination should be a symbol to the Jamaican churches to immaculate; and, end their present ongoing and developing squabbling among themselves.

5) The churches should see to the incorporation of Marcus's philosophies into the school curricula; they should pay special emphasis to his teachings as they relate(d) to *religion*; *Africa's redemption/ liberation* (e.g. South Africans/Southern Africans struggles against apartheid); *the "Back-To-Africa vision"*; and *"the politics of liberation."* [182]

6) The church needs to further acquaint itself with Marcus Garvey's teachings, especially as they relate to the development of other "traditional churches," and their theistic foundations, e. g. local Black Churches as: **the Bedwardites** and **the Rastafari community** (in particular **the Nyahbinghi Order of His Majesty**).

There needs to be a prolonged reasoning between the ecumenical community and these Black Churches.

Many of these Black churches core theology and world views are not known; recorded; or, are not clearly revealed by literate sources.

These Black Churches are best understood from *the oral archives.....*

---

[181] See Amy Jacques Garvey, **Garvey and Garveyism**, p. 3l.

[182] The *author* has long advocated the incorporation of Marcus's teachings, especially as they relate to Southern Africa's struggles against apartheid: see E.S.P. Mc Pherson (Introduced and Compiled), **The Most Honorable "Marcus" upon South Africa/Azania**, pp. vii, xxi-xxii, from early as February 1984.

Author's Biography

The author of this well researched book, Everton Mc Pherson was born in Waterworks, Clarendon, .on the 24th of October, 1955. He is the son of Mr. Leonard Octavius & Mrs. Hermine Mc Pherson (both deceased in December of 1974 & January of 1975 - respectively).

He attended the Frankfield Primary School, Munro College in St. Elizabeth 1965-71, Stratford High School in Kingston (1971), Clarendon College 1971-74. He later gained his Bachelor of Arts degree with Honors in African and Caribbean History (Political Science and Sociology) at the University of the West Indies, Mona, in 1982.

The author has recently completed his M.Sc. in Sociology (of Development) (USA).

His publishing house, **the Ethiopian**/Black International Iyahbinghi Press was established by himself in 1984. *A few* of his publications are

- **"RASTA CHRONOLOGY" (1982)**
- **UGLY PRETORIA (1984)**
- **"BROTHER BEDWARD" (1984)**
- **SONG OF REDEMPTION (1984)**
- **"BROTHER BEDWARD" - A REASON GIVEN.... (1985)**
- **"'MARCUS' UPON SOUTH AFRICA"/ AZANIA (1985)**
- **A VOICE CRYING OUT IN THE WILDERNESS - A Marcus Mosiah Garvey Centenary Celebration Presentation** (1987)
- **...I WILL ARISE** (1990)
- **RASTAFARI AND POLITICS: Sixty Years of a Developing Cultural Ideology. A Sociology of Development Perspective** (1991)
- **"MY GENERATION WILL MAKE THE CHANGE"... (1991**
- **A Message of Hope and Deliverance for Grassroots People in Jamaica (and the Caribbean)** (1993- **The Role of the Revolutionary Ethiopianist Intellectual...** (1994)
- **THE CULTURE-HISTORY AND UNIVERSAL SPREAD OF RASTAFARI: TWO Essays** (1994)
- **Has Rasta A Developmental Model for the Caribbean** (1990)
- **THE ETHNOHISTORY OF THE RASTAFARI CULTURE: Youth Black Faith: Nyahbinghi Order of His Majesty** (1994)

- **PAN-ETHIOPIANIZATION** (1994)
- **Jamaica (& The Ethio-Americas) - THE NEW ALTERNATIVE: A People's Revolution; A Human Time-Bomb** (1994)
- **INSIDE AZANIA (south africa)...** (1994)
- **TEACH - THE WAY FORWARD... (1994)**
- **ETHIOPIA: ONE NATION, MANY PEOPLES... (1994)**
- **THE CULTURE-HISTORY & UNIVERSAL SPREAD OF RASTAFARI... (1997)**

- **RASTAFARI:** ***The People's Theology from 'Below' Hermeneutic Interpretation; An Open Challenge to 'The Church'*** (Sept. 92/Oct. 94)

- **KULUNGU - TRADITIONAL RASTAFARI KUMINA SONGS, PRAYERS & REASONING OF THE HOWELLITES THE FIRST RASTAFARI COMMUNITY... (1996)**

- **HAILE SELASSIE 1/THE FIRST IS THE FIRE OF THE ATOM: RASTAFARI IN AMENTA (THE AMERICAS) (1997)**

- **...to begin the Reclamation of Our Ethiopian Sovereignty...**(1997)

- **THE ETHIO-DIASPORA CRY!... (1998)**

- **RASTAFARI & RASTAOLOGY (1998)**

- **L.I.O.N. - LIBERTY IN OUR NATION... (1998)**

- **TOWARDS THE CREATION OF A LEGISLATIVE AGENDA: CULTURAL SOLIDARITY THROUGH CULTURAL DIVERSITY** (1996)

- **ALL L.I.O.N. (LIBERTY IN OUR NATION) WILL RETURN: RASTAFARI - A CONTINENTAL FEDERAL FORMULA** (Nov. 3, 97/July 99)

- **ETHIOPIAN SOVREIGNITY & AFRICAN NATIONHOOD: VOICES FROM THE ETHIO-DIASPORA CALL...** (May 1994/ August 1999)

FROM ADDIS ABABA TO HARLEM: An Ethio-Rastafari International Perspective of The Million Youth March/M.Y.M. (July-September 98/Sept., 99.)

Ras E.S.P. Mc Pherson is a pro-active Cultural Activist and is currently Founder Chairman of the National Anti-apartheid Movement: A Southern African Working Committee (**NAM**); Ilect of Throne of The Nyahbinghi Order of His Majesty Rastafari International Coordinating Working Committee (**RICWC**); Founder and Co-Chairman of the Ethiopia Jamaica Society (**EJS**) - New York Chapter (**EJSNY**); Co-Chairman of Mo-Anbessa (**MOA**) - Jamaica/New York Chapters (The

Conquering Lion Organizing Committee); **Negusa Nagast** [Deputy Grand Master] of the Queen of Sheba & Pharaohs Masonic Movement (**QS&PMM**) - Education & Research Foundation; Co-Chairman of the Ethiopian Holocaust (Remembrance) Committee - New York Chapter (**EHRC**); Founder, Chairman of the **Ethiopian National Front (ENF) - Education & Research, Arts & Science Foundation**.

Ras Everton is also a free-lance Journalist. He has written for **The Jamaica Record, The Daily Gleaner, The Herald (Ja.)**, and a number of magazines globally, and international newspapers as **GAFFATA ETHIOPIA** (USA/Ethiopia); **Ethiopian Review** (USA) **The Ethiopian Examiner; City Sun** (NY); **Caribbean Life** (NY); **Daily Challenge** (NY) and magazines. He also contributes to a number of international Journals, and is *Editor* for a number of international Newsletters and Journals, as **Youth Black Faith/YBF: Order of the Nyahbinghi Journal Circular** (Jamaica); **National Anti-Apartheid Movement (NAM) Circular; Ethiopia Jamaica Society - New York Newsletter; Ethiopian National Front Circular**; and **Ethiopic News Watch Journal**.

As an educator and internationalist, this Cultural-Guerrilla between 1992-9...., has carried out a very intensive lecture tour throughout the USA universities, media houses, Ethio-Rastafari Community and Cultural Communities.

Ras E. S. P. Mc Pherson is undisputedly one of Ethiopia's/Africa's - Ethio-Jamaica - most talented writer, historian, sociologist and political scientist.

[**R.A.S./Rastafarian Advisory Service**, U. K. (1988); *E.S.P.*, USA (1999).]

Ethiopian National Front - (ENF) Education & Research, Arts & Science Foundation Catalogue

- **FROM ADDIS ABABA TO HARLEM: An Ethio-Rastafari International Perspective of The Million Youth March/M.Y.M.**, (USA, July 17-19,1998-September 3, 1998, **THE DAILY CHALLENGE**; released September 5th, 1999)........

Forthcoming Publications

- **ETHIOPIA SHALL BE REDEEMED: And Her Rightful Heir Shall Sit Upon Her Throne; THE RESURRECTION OF THE ETHIOPIAN QUESTION - in another political phase of action.**
- ETHIOPIC NEWS WATCH JOURNAL, Vol. 1 No. 1.
- **From "THE BLACK CHURCHES..." - BOOK TWO**

Cassettes

- RASTAFARI & RASTAOLOGY: *The Meeting at 'The African Village Square', An Interview between* **Bro. Junior Jawara Blake**, *Host of* **"The African Village Square,"** on *Caribbean Entertainment Network/CEN, WRTN Radio Station,* New Rochelle, New York, USA, and **Ras E.S.P. Mc Pherson...**, (Sunday 5th, 1996; released March 1998).

Distribution Price: ....$ 6.50
Retail: ....$10 .00

- **...to begin the Reclamation of Our Ethiopian Sovereignty Tapes 1 & 2**, *An Interview between* **Ras Negus Dawit ['David']**, *Host of* **"Reggae Vibrations,"** and **Ras E.S.P. Mc Pherson...**, on **WHCR/Harlem Community Radio 90.3 FM**, 9 p.m.-12 p.m., City College, Harlem, New York, USA, Wednesday June 17, 1997 (; released June 1998).

DISTRIBUTION PRICE: ....$ 6.50
RETAIL: $10.00

CD's
Kulungu -

TRADITIONAL RASTAFARI KUMINA SONGS, PRAYERS AND REASONING OF THE HOWELLITES
THE FIRST RASTAFARI COMMUNITY.
VOL. 1 THE INITIATION &
VOL. 2 THE HOWELLITES MEET THE NYAHBINGHI (Double C. D's)

Double set: $40
Vol.1 only: $20
Vol.2 only: $20

With a **72 pages** Introduction entitled: **"Honoring Our Original Ancestors: A Royal Ethiopic Salute To `The Gong'/The Howellites - A Introduction to Kulungu... Vols.1-4"**
Note, this is accompanied by two Transcripts (**96 pgs**) of the proceedings.

WRITE TO: Ras E.S.P. Mc Pherson,
Ethiopian National Front - (ENF)
Education & Research, Arts & Science Foundation,
c/o, 2507 Holland Avenue,
Bronx, New York, 10467,
U.S.A.
Phone: 1-718-547-6633; or: 1-917-362-5493
E-MAIL: kumina@tbol.net
WEBSITE: http://members.tripod.com/~rastaology

Index

A

K

L

M

R

S

T